Believing God's Word

Contents

Dedication

This book is dedicated to our Lord Jesus Christ, through Whose suffering, death and resurrection we have complete redemption. He brought us back to God.

Acknowledgement

I would like to thank all the wonderful people who encouraged me to write this book, and to finish it!

I would especially like to thank my brother, Gene, and my daughter, Amy, for their hard work in proofreading and correcting and critiquing this book. They made it much better. If you find any flaws, they are mine.

Preface

The most remarkable thing we have on Planet Earth is the Bible. There is nothing in God's great creation that compares with God's Word; after all, this is God talking to us, His created ones. Man cannot produce anything comparable to God's Word. Nothing more useful, nothing more wise, nothing more grand, nothing that has been made equals the importance and the beauty of the Bible. The writings of other religious books do not even come close to the beauty, wisdom and power of His Book. This is His Divine Gift.

God uses His Word to bring us close to Him. It is truly sent from Heaven for our benefit. God has sent only three things to us: His Son, His Spirit, and His Word. This book is about His Word.

As you read this little book, think about this wonderful gift and put it in your hands - daily. Consider what God's Word says, think on its truths. Let it dwell richly in your mind, heart and soul. May my little book help you accomplish this. Amen.

Importance of the Word of God

What did Jesus say about the Word of God?

Jesus said, "*It is written: Man must not live on bread alone but on every word that comes from the mouth of God.*" (Matthew 4:4). He was quoting Deuteronomy 8:3 where Moses was recounting the time when the Israelites were hungry and complaining. God then provided them 'manna' from heaven as their daily food for several years thereafter. Jesus used this food from Heaven as a type or metaphor to show our complete dependence on God and His Word for our sustenance, both physical and spiritual.

To Jesus, the Word of God is of paramount importance. In the Gospels, Jesus kept saying that Scripture must be fulfilled about Him and His work. *"Then He told them, 'These are My words that I spoke to you while I was still with you—that everything written about Me in the Law of Moses, the Prophets, and the Psalms must be fulfilled.'"* (Luke 24:44) He also said in John 10:35 that *"... Scripture cannot be broken."*

Jesus based His entire life on the Word of God. In fact, Jesus is the epitome of relying on God's Word. We can easily see this when we read the four Good News Letters: Matthew, Mark, Luke and John. For example, when Jesus was suffering on the cross and about to die, Matthew 27:46 says, *".... Jesus cried out with a loud vice, 'Eli, Eli, Lema sabachthani?"* he was quoting the first verse of Psalm 22, which depicts the crucifixion and the glory afterward. (If you read Psalms 22, 23 and 24 at one sitting, you will see the crucifixion, resurrection and glory that follows.)

Our Lord Jesus, Creator of the world, having come from Heaven as a man, depended entirely on the Word of God and

He fulfilled the Word of God. So then, how ought we to take the Scriptures? How important should they be in our lives? Shouldn't we too know the Word of God in order to fulfill God's destiny for us, *"All Scripture is inspired by God and is profitable for teaching, for rebuking, for correcting, for training in righteousness,"* (2 Timothy 3:16). We, just as Jesus, need to live in obedience to God's ways, in order to please God and to live the abundant, overcoming life that Jesus promised. (John 10:10; 16:33; I John 4:4).

Why the Word of God is Important to You

God's Word is important for many reasons, too many to list here, but here is a short list that I believe is central to our Christian living.

First, God's Word is true. Everything God says is true. From Genesis 1:1 "*In the beginning*" to Revelation 22:20-21 *"Amen! Come, Lord Jesus! The grace of the Lord Jesus be with all the saints."* In a world full of ideas, philosophies, opinions and feelings, God's Word is the standard for truth. Whatever doesn't agree with God's Word is wrong. Freud, Buddha, Mohammad, evolutionists, existentialists - wherever they disagree with God's Word, they are wrong. We can always rely on the veracity of God's Word.

Secondly, God's Word saves us! Romans 10:17 says that *"faith cometh by hearing and hearing by God's Word."* The way of Salvation, the most wonderful gift of God, is explained in His Word. Mankind has invented so many false ways to salvation, but the Word of God gives us the true way of salvation, which is completely by grace through faith in our risen Savior, Jesus Christ, God's only begotten Son. He died on the cross to pay for our sins. For God says, *"The wages of sin is death..."*. When we ask Him for forgiveness, He can forgive us because He rose from the dead and lives to help us, and He personally paid our judgement. No works, no striving - just turning back to God.

Thirdly, the Word of God helps us grow to be holy in following God's way. Jesus said in His great priestly prayer, *"Sanctify them by truth. Your Word is truth."* (John 17:17). 'Sanctify' means 'to make holy'. And the more one reads the Bible the more one has faith, and the more one has faith, the more one wants to follow God's way of doing the right thing.

Also, in the same vein, the Spirit of God cleanses us through the Word of God. The deeper the Word of God goes into my soul, the more putrid and ugly things it reveals in us. Then the Spirit of God convicts us of these sins and we confess them and receive a washing away of them. For, *"If we confess our sins, He is faithful and righteous to forgive us our sins and to cleanse us from all unrighteousness."* (I John 1:9). We become purer, more holy. And we become happier, more loving and considerate!

God uses His Word to change our lives. (Romans 12:2). To impart faith to our hearts. (Romans 10:17). To cleanse us. (John 15:3). To guide us. (Psalm 119:105). To correct us. (II Timothy 3:16). It shows us who God is and describes His character. It tells us about the Savior. It tells us how to get back to God. It is the perfect book for mankind. The Spirit of God wrote this out of His love for us, like a father helping his young children grow to become the very best they can be, full of life and goodness.

Fourthly, The Word of God guides us. Psalm 119:105 says, *"Your Word is a lamp for my feet and a light on my path."* George Muller, the great man of faith who accomplished so much just by prayer in England in the 1800s said that when he sought the will of God, he always made sure it was in accordance with Scripture. Such importance did he have in the veracity of the Word. The Word of God is deep in instructing us in His Ways. For example, the Book of Proverbs is full of practical wisdom, as are the letters of the New Testament. You will find practical teachings on following God and living life in every book of the Bible.

The Promises of God, Who Cannot Lie

Fifthly, the Words of God are the promises of God. He will never go back on His Word. The Word of God is trustworthy; we should remember that faith relies on the One Who said it. Our faith is in God; therefore, we trust what He says. It is not a magical book where we can claim whatever we want. Rather, it is a book that leads us to love and obey God and love our neighbor as ourselves and to keep ourselves pure.

These are but a few of the many reasons that the Word of God is important. But these few reasons should suffice in revealing to us the importance of God Word for our lives. After all, He wrote it for us. So, we should read it, daily.

Prayer: Heavenly Father, thank You for your Word You gave to us. Help us to understand how important it is in our lives. In Jesus glorious name we pray. Amen.

Power of the God's Word

What the Word of God Can Do

"For the word of God is alive and active. Sharper than any double-edged sword, it penetrates even to dividing soul and spirit, joints and marrow; it judges the thoughts and attitudes of the heart." Hebrews 4:12

When one thinks of power, one thinks of a force so strong that it causes change. The machine that drives huge pilings into the ocean floor, the monster trucks in the arena, a hurricane hitting the coast, Andre the Giant wrestling Hulk Hogan. And all these are powerful indeed, but there is a power that makes all these insignificant. The power of the Word of God. It penetrates our innermost being. That's power.

One day a short while ago, I was reading the Bible, as is my custom, and I came across this verse: *"Behold what manner of love the Father has bestowed on us, that we should be called children of God! Therefore, the world does not know us, because it did not know Him."* (1 John 3:1 NKJV).

I started thinking about this verse and what it really means. That in itself was the work of the Holy Spirit. He leads us along the still waters and pleasant pastures as Psalm 23 says. The Holy Spirit led me to dwell on this passage to better understand the meaning.

Then this verse has finally came alive to me. I have seen and read and believed this verse for over 40 years. But it never came alive to me. That ever happened to you? You read a verse, sometimes for years, and you believe it, and your belief in it is true. But it doesn't warm your soul. Your innermost being hasn't comprehended it and it is not yet part of your soul. That happens to me and I am sure it happens to you as well.

Yesterday evening, I read First John chapters three and four and two verses finally came alive. The first is the verse quoted above. I had always believed it, I had always trusted it, but it wasn't in my soul. Last night it came alive in my heart, not just the intellectual truth; it warmed my heart. It made me terribly happy. I smiled the smile of a person experiencing heavenly joy, a truly wonderful feeling. John Bunyan talks about this phenomenon several times in his book, *"Grace Abounding to the Chief of Sinnes."*

God has many, many times given me verses to help me in my life as I am sure He has for you as well. During my devotional readings, often a verse will pop out with a new facet of its meaning, like a diamond being look at from a different angle.

I see a separate facet, and I tuck it away in my mind as another wonderful truth God has shown me. I have several Bibles all marked up with underlines, highlights, notes and other types of markings (and a few squigglies). But when God implants His Word on our hearts, its different. It makes us wonder what we have been missing all this time. Now, in my heart, soul and mind, I know that I am God's child. I don't have to 'believe' (i.e., think it mentally and claim it with my own strength), I know. It's part of my psych now. As the apostle Paul said in 2 Timothy 1:12, *"I know the One I have believed in..."*

For sure the Spirit has borne witness before fulfilling Romans 8:16, *"The Spirit Himself testifies together with our spirit that we are God's children."* But for some reason this assurance is deeper. It's a part of me now. All my thinking about myself, my insecurities, my negative thinking, and my self-worth all vanished when God put it in my heart that I am His true child. (It comes back from time to time, like a single drop of rain on a sunny day, but now it just evaporates.) I really can't explain it more than this, except to say it's life changing. This particular truth of being God's child makes me smile when I go to sleep. It makes me happy whenever I think of it. It upholds my soul when bad or negative things happen or cross my mind. It is part of me now.

Missing the Blessing

But I might have missed this blessing if I had not dwelt on it and thought about it until I realized the truth of it. Not just a passing thought, but a deep, meditative consideration. A key to have the power of the Word of God permeate you, change you, and bless you is to think deeply on that verse that pops out to you. To think about it until it lights up your soul and gladdens your heart. It may take days or months. It is like a treasure in a field; it may take some digging to find it, but it is worth it.

God Accomplishes His Word

Jeremiah 1:12 says, "*I watch over My word to accomplish it.*" God's Word, the Bible, has power, not just power to motivate one's actions, but power to transform lives, to raise us from spiritual death into being born again, (Titus 3:5-6). God will fulfill all that is in the Bible, all prophecies, promises and judgements. God's Word is backed by His power! If God says that He will make Israel a nation again, He will make Israel a nation again. If God says He will forgive all who come to Him, He will accomplish His Word and forgive.

Our Choice

God also desires and requires us to choose to accomplish His Word. Our free will God will not abuse. When the angel of the Lord spoke to Mary about her upcoming pregnancy, Mary responded, "*I am the Lord's slave,* said Mary. *May it be done to me according to your word.*" (Luke 1:48) Mary co-operated by giving God permission to do this mighty work in her.

We, too, must acquiesce to God's plan for our lives, else we will be out of God's will for our lives. We won't be all that we can be for God. We will miss the blessing and more importantly, we will miss serving Christ as He wishes us to serve Him. And that would be a sad life to live. So, let's not miss the blessing.

Don't Miss the Blessing

There are many passages in the Bible that I believe. In fact, I believe the whole Bible! The problem is that I don't yet know what they mean or the depth of what they mean. For example, in Matthew 5:14, Jesus said, *"You are the light of the world."* To find out how well I know it, I have to explain it to someone. And I don't do a very good job with this verse. I know it, I read it, I believe it, but I simply don't know it to the degree that I think I should. In my mind and my heart, I believe it, but I haven't yet experienced it. I know it to some extent that I should do good works to glorify my Father

(Matthew 5:16), but I think it goes deeper than that. It doesn't live in my soul yet. My soul doesn't fully comprehend its meaning because the Holy Spirit hasn't imprinted it on my soul yet. Maybe I haven't given Him the opportunity to. It could be that I am not ready for the depth of that truth, but I think more is the case that I simply haven't devoted enough time to meditate and pray about this truth.

However, once the Word of God is embedded by the Spirit of God into your heart and soul, and not just in your mind, it changes your soul. The Holy Spirit is working in your soul. Through the Word of God, He conforms you more to the image and character of Jesus Christ, which should be the goal of all Christians.

Be more like Jesus

We are to be ever increasingly more like Christ, who dwells in us. *"For those He foreknew He also predestined to be conformed to the image of His Son."* (Romans 8:29). His Spirit, the Holy Spirit, is always working to change us for the better. We must be willing. And we must meditate on God's Word. Maybe it's a truth God has shown you years earlier and you have neglected to keep it in your heart. Maybe it is a new revelation that God has shown you this morning. Either way, let it sink into your heart. Meditate upon it, ask God about it until God gives you the smile of knowing how great His love is. And you'll know when it sinks into your heart because you become happy (blessed) in your soul. This also is the power of God's Word.

For example, the verse God gave me yesterday evening was *"There is no fear in love; but perfect love casts out fear, because fear involves torment. But he who fears has not been made perfect in love."* (I John 4:18 NKJV). I understand the context of this verse but allow me to put forth the idea that this verse is a universal truth, a truth that God, who does not lie, has given us for our edification. You see, I was having difficulty with an upcoming event. I was worried that things would go badly, especially based on what I knew about my own character and the event I was going to attend.

And then I read this verse and realized in my heart that 'there is no fear in love'. It came to me that Jesus loves me completely. It was as if Jesus was telling me, "If you keep your eyes on me, because I love you and will be with you and will take care of you." Once I realized was Jesus was telling me through the Holy Spirit, I lost all worry, ... and smiled. Jesus loves me. He has my situation in total control. But to believe this, I must keep my focus, my mind, my spiritual eyes on Him. If I don't, unbelief sets in. Just like when Peter was walking on the water. Then worry comes again, then situations get the best of me, and problems arise. I begin to sink. But the joy of keeping my eyes on Jesus is so much better!

The upcoming event, now over, was a blast! One little hitch came along when worry set in. If I had rebuked that worry (for worry is not of God), that would not have happened the way it did. But it was just a little hiccup during that fun day. By exercising our faith we can keep our eyes on Jesus. Faith is like a muscle, the more you use it, the stronger it gets. This allows us to keep our eyes on Jesus more and more.

The truth that 'perfect love casts out all fear' was embedded in my heart and soul, not just stuck in the intellect. Knowing God's truths in my soul and heart brings hope and joy, not just mental agreement, but JOY!

The power of God's Word can do anything. Miracles are no problem with God. In fact, I believe that what we consider miracles, God considers these to be natural. To God, walking on water, natural, feeding of the 5,000, natural. Resurrection of the dead? Natural. No situation is too complicated or too difficult. But the biggest power of God's Word is the change it makes in your soul.

The Sword of the Lord

"For the Word of God is alive and powerful. It is sharper than the sharpest two-edged sword, cutting between the soul and spirit, between the joints and marrow. It exposes our innermost thought and desires." (Hebrews 4:12).

"A final word: Be strong in the Lord and in His mighty power. Put on all of God's armor so that you will be able to stand firm against all the strategies of the devil. For we are not fighting against flesh and blood enemies, but against evil rulers and authorities of the unseen world, against mighty powers in this dark world, and against evil spirit in the heavenly places."..."Put on salvation as your helmet, and take the sword of the Spirit, which is the Word of God." (Ephesians 6:10-12,17).

God gave us His Word to use. Mythology has Thor's hammer; fairy tales have King Arthur's Excalibur, but we have the real thing, the most powerful weapon given to man - the Word of God. You are called by God to use it. Practice your swordsmanship! Do you know the Word of God well enough to use it? This and prayer are the weapons of choice by God. Let us become skilled warriors.

Ways to Use the Sword of God

One way I have found how to use this powerful weapon: If, as you read the Bible and find some passage that promises one thing, like good health, and you don't have it, ask God why. And then, listen for His answer. He promises to reveal it to you, if you wait on Him. Psalm 84:11 says, *"... He does not withhold the good from those who live with integrity."* God will reveal it to you. It may be through the Word of God, or through circumstances, or possibly through a person, or directly to you. However God reveals this to you, act on it. This is where your faith becomes believing. Jesus gives us victory, but we must believe Him. We must seek His wisdom. Remember when Paul asked the 'thorn in his side' to be taken away. God replied to his prayers, *"My grace us sufficient for you, for my power is made perfect in weakness."* (2 Corinthians 12:9).

When God, the Holy Spirit, impresses on your heart to claim a certain verse, claim it! If God says to pray and you will be healed, pray and claim it! If God says go see the doctor, go see the doctor! Both ways, its God healing. If God says His grace is sufficient for you, live with it. In other words, when God gives you a verse, use that verse as the Sword of the Lord!

A Word of Warning

But let's be careful that we don't make ourselves into a 'god'. Contrary to what some name-it-claim-it teachers that believers follow, God does indeed allow us to suffer for reasons that may only be known to Him. And for those folks who claim prosperity always, I suggest they go live in Nigeria or Saudi Arabia or China and teach that there!

God does heal. God does cause prosperity. But to command this to happen in every circumstance is an ugly false belief that has hurt many good Christians. It makes man god and God a tool to be used as man sees fit. So, beware of this false teaching. They are easy to spot. They focus and certain verses and never bring up other verses that contradict their teaching. And often they focus on money. Hmmm. When Jesus focused on money, His take was quite different, wasn't it? I don't think Jesus ever wore a Rolex.

Stopping The Tempter's Lies

The evil one takes great pleasure in tempting us to sin, which tarnishes our reputation among those he is hiding the Good News from and it hinders our fellowship with Christ.

The lies are simple sentences. For example, This is good for me. Or, One slip won't hurt me. Or, No one will know. Or, I'm tired of striving, I'm going to give in just a little bit.

Sound familiar? It does to me! And how many times I have fallen for those tricks of Satan, our enemy. He seduces us into thinking it is okay to sin a little. TV ads are full of these selfish temptations; Just Do It! Have it your way! You deserve a break to day!, etc. ad nauseam.

When these temptations come up, compare them to the Word of God. That's what Jesus did! If you do that, you will save yourself much grief. The Word of God is true and anything that goes against it (in context) is of the devil. The Sword of the Spirit will keep you safe when you use it.

Are You a Good Swordsman?

I have a nine-millimeter Smith and Wesson in my home. If I just let it lie there and never practice with it, how good of a shot do you think I will be? Can I hit what I am aiming at? Probably not. I have to practice keeping it steady, trigger pull, sighting, etc. It is the same with the Sword of the Spirit, which is the Word of God. If you don't use it, you will be a lousy swordsman! So, get into the practice of wielding your Sword whenever you can. Cut through the lies of Satan. Stab the falsehood with the truth. Cut off the head of the serpent's false idea by proclaiming the truth. Know the truth!

We are fighting against the world and its satanic, selfish systems, the flesh (our own sin nature) and the devil who wants to destroy us. How effectively will you fight without a weapon? Use the Word of God. It is your weapon and it is very powerful.

Prayer: Almighty God, You truly can do anything. You even said You will do more than we ever thought, *"Now to Him who is able to do exceedingly abundantly above all that we ask or think, according to the power that works in us,"* Eph. 3:20 NKJV. Work in our hearts to meditate on your Word, especially the truths you reveal to us, until they sink deep into our hearts and permeate our souls with truth, hope and joy. And then, Lord, help us to use Your Word as you intended. In the Name above all names, the glorious Name of your Son, Jesus the Christ, Lord of the Universe, we pray, Amen!

Positiveness of God's Word

The Biggest Influencer in the World

God's Word is a positive influence in the World. It affirms that we have a hope and a future. It affirms that morality is good and that loving God and loving each other is the highest morality.

Yet, there are many people who believe that the word of God is negative. After all, it talks about evil, wars, judgment, among other things. Usually, the people who have a negative view of the Bible haven't read the Bible. But some have and, unfortunately, there are some preachers and other Christians who seem to go along with the negative aspect of the Bible. So, let's look at why some people, Christians and non-Christians, see the Bible as negative and then let's explore why those who actually love God and read the Bible see it as the most positive book ever written. We'll look at both sides and see what's what.

What People Say When They Knock the Bible

First the negative. The Bible says we are sinners, and that is a bad thing. In fact, it is so bad that God says we must go to hell, the lake of fire that burns forever. The Bible says each of us will have our own personal judgement day. Hebrews 9:27 states, *"And just as it is appointed for people to die once – and after this, judgment."* That's rather negative, isn't it?

Also, Ezekiel 18:4 states, *"The person (soul) who sins is the one who will die."* And Romans 3:23 reads, *"For all have sinned and fall short of the glory of God."* And according to Revelation 21:8, *But the cowards, unbelievers, vile, murderers, sexually immoral, sorcerers, idolaters, and all liars*

- their share will be in the lake of fire that burns with fire and sulphuric, which is the second death." So, putting these three verses together, every one of us is destined for death, eternal judgment and the second death which certainly includes a complete separation from God and His goodness forever. Very negative that!

The second point some people like to bring up is: what about God's commands to the Israelites as they begin to enter Canaan to take possession of the land? They were commanded to destroy every man, woman and child and baby. In some cases, even the livestock was to be destroyed completely. (I Samuel 15:3). How can a moral God justify this?

Thirdly, and probably the biggest complaint about the Bible is that it says there is only one way to Heaven. People are constantly attacking Christians because Christians say there's is the only way to Heaven.

People reject this idea as excluding all those nice people who follow a different path to Heaven. Buddhists, Muslims, Hindi, the non-religious morally upright. In fact, people get downright angry when they hear there is only one way. Oprah speaks out against there being one way, and she says she is a Christian. The argument goes like this: My neighbor is a good person and is spiritual. She doesn't believe in Jesus but she is good. Surely God, who is fair, will accept her, won't He? I believe Oprah and many others take this view.

These seem to be strong arguments for looking at the Bible and Christians in a negative light. However, let's explore these ideas and see if these arguments hold up.

On the Flip Side

Let's now look at these arguments from the positive side of the Bible and see which best describes reality. First, God created the earth and mankind and proclaimed His creation of the earth and all that is in it 'good' and once man was created, things weren't just 'good', but 'very good'. (Genesis 1:31). In fact, He said He created mankind in His image. (Genesis 1:26). Therefore, God created a good world and we humans were even created in His good image. This is the first positive.

After man rebelled against God, broke His holy law and brought evil (selfishness and self-worship) to mankind, He immediately provided a way for mankind to be brought back, to be restored just as if they had never sinned (i.e., breaking God's law is called sin, i.e. being a law breaker).

Genesis 3:15 give us the beginning of the Positive News of God's Plan. To the serpent who deceived Eve, who then tempted Adam, God said, *"I will put hostility between you and the woman, and between your seed and her seed. He will strike your head and you will strike his heel."* This promise was fulfilled in Jesus Christ, God's only Son. Colossians 2:14-15 says, *"He erased the certificate of debt, with its obligations, that was against us and opposed to us, and has taken it out of the way by mailing it to the cross. He disarmed the rulers and authorities and disgraced them publicly; He triumphed over them through the cross."* (i.e., crushing the Serpents head).

The cross, of course, is the cross that Jesus died and shed His blood on. This is a very positive thing! Jesus set up free from the power of sin and death. (Romans 8:2) The devil who had enslaved us was stripped of His power to enslave us and was completely defeated. We can be free from the evil one! The devil who had enslaved us in sin, thereby corrupting the image of God in us, lost his hold on us when Jesus paid our debt for us. As Ezekiel 18:4 states, *"The person (soul). that sins is the one who will die."* But Jesus paid the price with His death for each of us who sinned! Rather positive, don't you think?

Another positive is that God stops evil! Just think if God didn't stop evil! Chaos and terror would rule the day, every day. It would be a dysfunctional, dystopian world, even more so than it is now. A world of only greed, fear, pain, and suffering. But God hates evil and He stops evil from taking over! Evil does exist in the world because people do evil things, but evil can only go so far in this world because God restrains evil from taking over (II Thessalonians Chapter 2).

Each person has his or her individual choice to do evil or not, but God has set a limit on how much evil can be done. The Genesis Flood is an example of this. At that time, people's evil actions reached a point where God stepped in and proclaimed judgement and stopped the evil. The Giver of Life took the lives of those who kept doing evil in life and would not turn to Him. As Job rightly says, *"The Lord gives, and the Lord takes away. Praise the name of the Lord (Yahweh)."*

As I write, evil is increasing in the world dramatically. Murders are way up, violent crimes in most major cities are up, etc. People seem to be eager to throw off the yoke of being good and instead are seeing how selfish they can be. Victimhood is the new politics of the day. Entitlement and selfishness abound. God is patient, hoping people will turn to Him, but His patience has a limit. The book of Revelation shows us that limit. When someone turns to God, he or she quits doing evil, quits hating people, quits stealing, quits judging others, quits drunkenness or drugs, etc. Whoever turns back to God, receives God's goodness back in their heart. Very positive, that! Evil is caused by man, but goodness comes from God. God offers each of us a way to stop our own evil and He has limits on what he will tolerate.

Evil is Always Judged

Let's look at 1 Samuel 15 where God told Israel to destroy completely the Amalekites. In Exodus 18:8 and following we read how the Amalekites attacked the Israelites when they were weary from their travels. This was completely unprovoked. They were even relatives of the Hebrews as they were descendants of Esau, the brother of Jacob. And God vowed to wipe them out, Exodus 17:14. So, there was a reason for God's wiping them out. And another point, even more significant, is that God is the Creator of mankind and He who created life has the right to take life. It is in His judgment as the Creator and King to reward good and punish evil.

Also, there was another group, the Amorites. We read in Genesis 15:16 *"In the fourth generation they* (the Israelites) *will return here* (Caanan), *for the iniquity of the Amorites has not yet reached its full measure."* The nations in that land that the Hebrews were to inherit, were very bad people. They practiced all kinds of evil against each other and were sexual perverts to the nth degree. In fact, those disgusting sexual acts were part of their religious service! God gave them time to repent and turn from their evil ways, but instead they became full of their sins and God finally judged their evil through the invading Israelites, though He was patient wanting not even one to perish (2 Peter 3:9). Can God use people to stop evil? Of course! That God stops evil is in itself a very positive thing.

Who has the Right to Judge?

I am sure of two things in life. First, no one knows all the facts. Secondly, God is good and He does know all the facts.

Therefore, we should not judge God based on our own limited knowledge. No one has all the facts. In fact, we still can't answer God's questions in the oldest book of the Bible, the book of Job. Today's astrophysicists have some facts and many theories. Right now, I am watching Dr. Russ Hughs, a Christian astrophysicist, describe how it took 14 billion years, according to physics, to prepare the earth for life. I listen to him, but I don't understand much of what he says. But Dr. Hughs stated in another video I watched that according to physics and dimensions, etc., God has to be a trillion trillion times smarter than man to do what He did.

So, if God is so much smarter than us, how can we call Him evil when we don't know all the facts? If we don't have all the facts, how can we judge correctly? Well, you might say that we see evil all around us. When you look closely at evil, you will see that it is man-made and not from God.

It really comes down to faith. Do you have faith in the goodness of God, or do you have faith in yourself to be the judge of the earth? You must decide.

Another point is: What about this second death? That is really negative! Tossed into a lake of fire that burns forever? Yet, for God to be good, there must be a hell. Hell is real and the second death is real. A holy God, a good God, cannot put up with sin, otherwise known as evil. He will separate evil from Himself and His kingdom. He calls this separation hell. The second death destroys evil for good. More on this later.

Now, let's take a brief look at the character of God.

A Good Character Must Judge Evil

The Ten Commandments reveal the character of God. First, in the Ten Commandments, we must respect the true God and don't worship anyone or anything else. One of the reasons for this is that if we do worship something else, we harm ourselves because we change the character of God in our minds to something not as good as God. We follow what we worship so we end up doing very bad things. For example, if one makes consumerism her god, then she will live to consume, which puts her on a selfish, self-destructive course.

Secondly, God is to be respected; this is called worship (i.e. counted worthy of our respect). He made our bodies, souls and spirits. He deserves our respect.

Next, the Ten Commandments tells us how God wants us to treat each other. Don't murder, lie against someone, etc. Jesus, God's Son, summed it up this way, *"Therefore, whatever you want others to do for you, do also the same for them - this is the Law and the Prophets* (i.e., Old Testament)*."* (Matthew 7:12). This shows that the character of God is good. No other nation had a similar set of rules. God's rules reveal that God created man for goodness' sake.

By the Ten Commandments alone, we can see the good character of God. But there is more. The Bible says His goodness and mercy is with us every day as we follow Him (Psalm 23:6). and His love endures forever (Psalm 136:1). So, we see that God is good and if we think about it, we can see His goodness in action. Matthew 5:45 says, *"... For He causes His sun to rise on the evil and the good, and sends rain on the righteous and the unrighteous."* (By the way, this is God's morality, i.e. loving your neighbor as you love yourself, even when your neighbor is your enemy.) We have what we need, we have reason, community, beauty, pleasure, etc. These good things are all from God, designed for us from the creation of the world. These also show the goodness of God.

So, what about Hell?

First it is not God's desire to send anyone to Hell. In 1 Peter 3:9, God says, *"The Lord does not delay His promise, as some understand delay, but is patient with you, not wanting any to perish but all to come to repentance."* He gave each of us a way out! God has given every person a free will, the ability to choose to follow Him or not. (We are not robots programmed to follow Him. That would neither be love nor would it be good. If we were robots, we could not love, hate or have any other emotion. We would never have a choice or a will to choose. Freewill is the groundwork for all these characteristics and more.) Those who choose to follow Him have eternal life and an eternally good life. Those who prefer evil must be judged according to God's character which is pure and righteous. God does the right thing.

Abraham found this out when He met God's messengers who were on their way to destroy Sodom and Gomorrah. In Genesis 18 Abraham asks, *"Will You really sweep away then righteous with the wicked... You could not possibly do such a thing: to kill the righteous with the wicked, treating the righteous and the wicked alike."* (Genesis 18:24-25) Abraham knew God. He knew that God's character is impeachable. Abraham knew God's character was good. Abraham knew that God judges evil.

When evil is judged this is called the second death. This is for those to refuse to do good because they wish to do evil, rebelling against God and harming others. God, as the fair judge, must judge them according to their actions. Their actions condemn their own selves before the Righteous Judge.

But there is hope!

"The wages of sin is death, but the gift of God is eternal life through Jesus Christ our Lord." (Romans 6:23). Those

who refuse God's Way will suffer the second death. But God offers a way out! He doesn't want you to go to Hell. He planned Heaven for you.

John 3:16 clearly states God's plan and will for us, *"For God so loved the world* (you and me). *that He gave His one and only Son, so that everyone who believes in Him will not perish but have eternal life."* If God loves us to the extent that He asked His Son to suffer and take our wickedness on His body while dying on the cross, surely, He has, at great sacrifice to Himself and His Son, given us a way to happiness and life.

Romans 6:23 states that *"gift of God is eternal life in Christ Jesus our Lord."* And Romans 5:12 clearly shows how Jesus is able to save us, *"For if, while we were enemies, we were reconciled to God through the death of his Son, then how much more, having been reconciled, will we be saved by His Life!"* God's gift to us is eternal life with Him if we want it.

The way of salvation is open to all. This is even true for those who judge God as having evil motives. Have you, the skeptic who complains about God's fairness, asked God to create in you a clean heart by receiving forgiveness through His Son, Jesus? If not, why are you still judging God as evil? You haven't checked out His side of the issue.

How Many Ways to God Are There?

Finally, regarding the complaint against Christians that God's Word isn't right because there are many ways to God. Two things stand out. First, the idea that there are good people who deserve Heaven has been proven false. Which of you profess yourself to be good? IF you never sinned, you get to go to Heaven freely! But if you have broken God's law, God's way, you condemn yourself. As it says in Romans 3:10 *"... there is none righteous..."* And Romans 3:23 *"For all have sinned and fall short...of the glory of God."* Fall short of what? Of the glory of God, which is the goodness of God. (Exodus 38:18-19) Not one of us has been good like God, have we?

This is very easy to find out. Ask yourself these two questions: Do you love God with all your heart, your mind, and your will? Do you always love your neighbor as yourself? If you answer those two questions honestly, you will see that there is no truly good person according to God's standard of good. People can do good things, but that does not make them good. A murderer can open a door for a lady at the store but he is still a murderer. Good actions do not outweigh evil deeds.

Secondly, and most importantly, it is not for us to say how to approach God, it is at God's discretion. God sent His Son. God did not send another savior or devise another way. Jesus said, *"I am the way...".* Not a way, but The Way. Jesus also said, *"I have come in my Father's name..."* John 5:43. And, *"Jesus said to her,* (Martha). *"I am the resurrection and the life."* And in Acts 4:12 it sates, *"There is salvation in no one else, for there is no other name under heaven given to people, and we must be saved by it."* God sent His Son. Whoever comes to Jesus has eternal life. Christianity in not exclusive, but inclusive. Everyone is invited! It is Christ Himself who invites everybody to come to Him! Jesus is The Way.

The Positiveness of God's Word for Society

Now let's look at more of the positiveness of God's Word. How has it influenced individuals? Jesus transforms individual lives. He fills that empty void that is in the souls of every man. St. Augustine rightly said that the heart is not quiet till it rests in God for God has made us for Himself. God gives meaning to life. He forgives us and transforms us. There are literally hundreds of thousands of testimonies of how God has changed individual lives, families, and communities and even nations for the better. Now, that's positive!

Individuals interact with each other and this creates society and if individuals become better, then society becomes better because of individuals' interactions.

Christianity has given us the sanctity of life. Each life is precious according to the Bible. The one-time slave trader, John Newton, decided to follow Jesus Christ. He was a successful slave trader for several years, and actually became a slave once himself! He received forgiveness through Christ and renounced his trade and became an ardent supporter of the abolition of slavery, which he saw come to pass in England in 1807. (One of the greatest hymns of Christianity was written by him: Amazing Grace. The firsts words of the song are "*Amazing Grace how sweet the sound that save a wretch like me.*")

Christians have always worked for the freedom of their fellow man. The United States Declaration of Independence was directly influenced by the Bible when it said, *"All men are created equal .... Endowed by their Creator with unalienable Rights. .... Life, Liberty and the pursuit of Happiness."* The anti-slavery movement in American was started by Christians.

And there is much more: moral values, women's dignity, charity work, child labor laws, equal justice, morality, hospitals, etc. All these were propagated by Christians. St. Patrick changed the barbarism of Ireland to a country of peace (comparatively speaking).

Jesus has compassion and respect for every human being and His followers do too. If fact, if a professing Christian doesn't have compassion and respect for every human being, his claim on being a Christian is highly suspect. Christians follow Jesus. We are His disciples.

God's Word Gives a Positive Outlook

The Word of God gives us a positive outlook on life! After all, why worry when you have such promises as the following?

Jesus said in Matthew 6:25-34 that God will provide all our needs as we follow Him. Verses 33 and 34 states, *"But seek first the kingdom of God and all these things will be provided for you. Therefore, don't worry about tomorrow, because tomorrow will worry about itself. Each day has enough trouble."* And I Peter 5:7 states, *"casting all your care on Him, because He cares about you."* There are so many Scriptures that tell us not to fear because He will help us. Isaiah 41:10, *"Do not fear, for I am with you; do not be afraid because I am your God..."* For a world that lives constantly in fear: fear of war, fear of climate change, fear of violence, fear of what we eat, fear of so many things, what Jesus does is very positive! We can have life without fear; we can have a positive outlook on life! He wants us to fill us with the positives of love, joy and peace (Galatians 5:22).

Another positive aspect is that the Word of God tells us to help each other, to have compassion for each other. I Peter 3:8 says, *"all of you should be like-minded and sympathetic, should love believers, and be compassionate and humble"* and I John 3:16-18, *This is how we have come to know love; He laid down His life for us. We should also lay down our lives for our brothers. If anyone has this world's good and sees his brother in need but closes his eyes to his need - how can God's love reside in him? Little children, we must not love with word or speech, but with truth and action."* And finally, Jude 22, *"And on some have compassion, making a difference."* (NKJV). All this can be summed up in Jesus' Words, Matthew 7:12, *"Therefore, whatever you want others to do for you, do also the same for them."*

The Word of God Promises You a Good Life

God not only takes care of us, He guides us in this life. Jesus came to save us and give us a full and good life. John 10:10 shows why Jesus came, *"I have come so that they may have life and have it in abundance!"* That is positively Good News! He came to give us an abundant life, a life full of goodness. We will have hardships and trials, but throughout there will be joy unspeakable as we follow Jesus.

Proverbs 3:5-6 clearly explains how God helps us and guides us. *"Trust in the Lord with all your heart, and lean not on your own understanding. In all your ways acknowledge Him, and He shall direct your paths."* And Jeremiah 29:11, *"For I know the thoughts that I think toward you, says the Lord, thoughts of peace and not of evil, to give you a future and a hope."* God is for us. He wants the best for us as we live out our lives. Can't get more positive than that!

And beyond that, Jesus came that we might live forever! Romans 6:23 tells us that eternal life is our gift from God, *".... The gift of God is eternal life through Jesus Christ our Lord."* That is a very positive reality!

The Word of God is positive. God loves you and sent His Son Jesus to save you from your sins. Nothing on earth is as positive or powerful as that!

To sum up, when you read the Bible with an open mind, you will find that it is the most positive book in the world.

Prayer: Father, thank You for your goodness, love and mercy. Show us how positive You are toward each one of us. Show us how much you love us and care for us. In Jesus name, amen.

Understanding God's Word

Study, Study, Study

In 2 Timothy 2:15 it says, *"Be diligent to present yourself approved to God, a worker who does not need to be ashamed, rightly dividing the word of truth."* God tells us to study the Word carefully, to be diligent in our studies and to make sure we understand it rightly and to teach/preach it rightly. But I think many Christians, leaders included, are missing the mark, as I, myself, did for so many years.

Some of our Christian leaders are so focused on teaching their denominational or personal doctrines that they often forget that the doctrines are meant for us to love God and love each other deeply. In other words, they don't take it to the conclusion of the doctrine, the end result. To me, this is not rightly dividing the word of truth, but wrongly dividing the Word.

This happens especially when the pet teachings of particular denominations are always put forward in their preaching. Each denomination has its pet doctrines, the one they emphasize more than the others, the one that makes them 'special'. I have visited scores of churches and see it all the time.

This happened in New Testament times as well. Paul wrote to Timothy to tell those who strive about words to knock it off. It doesn't benefit anything toward godliness. In fact, Paul calls it 'babblings'! And in First Corinthians, people were dividing the church into personality cults of Paul, Peter, etc. "Oh, Peter's teaching is better. His doctrines are better than

Paul's!" So, this isn't something new, but it is something we should guard against.

Understand the Purpose of the Bible.

Even non-denominational churches often slide into their pet doctrines. It might be over-emphasizing the gifts of the Spirit, or under emphasizing grace. And many of us Christians have 'itchy ears' (2 Timothy 4:3). enjoying the prideful idea that we have the 'right' teachings. I have been there myself and know countless others who are caught in that trap as well. Is this pleasing to our Lord Jesus? No, it isn't. In fact, we grieve the Holy Spirit when we do this. So, the question arises: How do we counteract this?

The Purpose of Paul's Teachings

We must remind ourselves that the doctrines Paul taught had a purpose. 1 Timothy 1:5 says, *"Now the purpose of the commandment is love from a pure heart, from a good conscience, and from a sincere faith."* Paul was not pugnacious. He presented the truth and defended the truth but left a lot of room for grace. We, who are not Paul, need to realize that not one of us has perfect Bible knowledge, which means all of us are wrong in some areas. We need to remember that everything God does for us is motivated by love. We should emulate our Father and make sure love motivates our hearts. As we study the Word of God, we must have the proper motivation.

We can study and become scholars of the Bible, but miss the mark. I was talking to a gentleman last night whose father graduated from Princeton School of Divinity. The father was quite learned in the biblical languages, having mastered Greek, Hebrew and Aramaic. He was a pastor, but his heart was quite arrogant. He treated his children badly and even took his son on his excursions to find women! He brain focused on the Bible, but his heart focused on selfishness. *"Knowledge puffs up, but love builds up."* (1 Corinthians 8:1, ESV).

If I think I have the correct teaching on a matter, I try to just say it, or discuss it, once and not argue about it. I let the Holy Spirit do His work to convince or correct. And sometimes, I am the one who needs to be corrected!

Understand what you are reading

Another thing I have learned is that we need to meditate, to think about the Word of God. I once thought about Mathew 7:11 on and off for months. *"If you then, being evil, know how to give good gifts to your children, …."* I couldn't figure out how evil could do good as Jesus said. I wanted to know so that I could rightly God's Word. It was quite puzzling. After much studying and thinking and prayer, I realized that evil can do good because it doesn't affect their desire for evil. Evil can show goodness when it doesn't interfere with one's evil desires. For example, a murderer can open the door for a lady or change someone's tire, etc. They don't kill everybody they see. Because it doesn't negatively affect what they want. Evil is selfish, it attacks whatever threatens it, if possible. If not possible, it hides its agenda and smolders in envy, jealousy, hate, etc. It took me a long time to figure that out. But with the help of the Helper, the Holy Spirit, I did.

"And He personally gave some to be apostles, some prophets, some evangelists, some pastors and teachers, for the training of the saints in the work of the ministry, to build up the body of Christ," (Ephesians 4:11).

Just after I got saved, I had the opportunity to attend bible college. I learned much from very good teachers. Good teachers are a gift and a blessing. The Holy Spirit uses them to help us understand the Word of God and the ways of God. This implies that we need help to understand the Word of God and He gives us that help through teachers. Without teachers, there is a lot we don't know. Even the Apostle Peter said of the Apostle Paul, *"... just as our dear brother Paul has written to you according to the wisdom given to him. He speaks about these things in all his letters in which there are some matters that are hard to understand. The untaught and unstable twist them to their own destruction, as they also do with the rest of scripture."* (2 Peter 3:15-16).

Most of us don't have the time to study the Bible as we should. We have jobs, families, other responsibilities, etc. We do not have the time or wherewithal to learn Hebrew and Greek (let alone Chaldean or Aramaic) with the different grammar and word studies, etc. Do we understand how God acts in the Bible, the history surrounding the biblical narrative, the systematic study of God's ways and actions, the practical applications of God Way? I have personally been studying this for years and still feel like I am just scratching the surface.

As we found out, Peter himself said some of Paul's teachings were hard to understand. Peter the fisherman did not have the same educational background as Paul, the theologian. God used the theologian to write much of the teachings in the New Testament. In fact, God raised up Paul and put him through the school of Gamaliel, the great first century Jewish rabbi, for that very purpose.

Teachers are God's messengers to teach us about Him. But Peter and Paul both warn us to watch out for those teachers who are false, who twist God's Word for their own ends. *"But there were also false prophets among the people, just as there will be false teachers among you. They will secretly bring in destructive heresies, even (to the point) of denying their Master who bought them and will bring swift destruction on themselves. Many will follow their unrestrained ways, and the way of truth will be blasphemed because of them. They will exploit you in their greed with deceptive words."* (2 Peter 2:1-3) The Apostle Paul said in his farewell speech the church leaders at Ephesus, a very spiritual church, *"I know that after my departure savage wolves will come in among you, not sparing the flock. And men will rise up from your own number with deviant doctrines to lure the disciples into following them. Therefore, be on the alert..."* (Acts 20:29-31). Did you notice that these 'false teachers' always induce the Christian to follow, not Christ, but themselves?

So, we need teachers, but we must have the right teachers. This calls for prayer and wisdom. Questions we must ask about teachers are: Do they hold to the basic biblical and historical truths about Jesus, His death and resurrection? Are they bringing in doctrines that take us away from focusing on Jesus? Not good. Do they hold the Bible to be God's Word and not man's. Do they teach salvation by grace alone and not by works? Do they teach that the purpose of teaching about God is love and purity? *"Now the goal of our instruction is love that comes from a pure heart, a good conscience, and a sincere faith."* (I Timothy 1:5).

When I lived in Korea, there in my neighborhood was a small church on the second floor of a corner building. The young minister and his wife loved people and showed it in their witnessing about Jesus. They developed various ways to witness to people. He talked with me one day. I asked him what his church was doing and he lit up and said they were passing out tracts and witnessing to those in the area, etc. I then asked him about the church across the corner and he told me that they had moved in after his church started. They were focusing on the gifts and not the Giver and were pulling people away from his church.

Whenever a teacher's main focus is on anything but Jesus and where there is no real love, that is a false teacher. There are a bunch of them in your town and a bunch on TV as well. Beware and choose wisely and prayerfully. Does their teaching promote love for God, hate for sin and mercy for all as Micah 6:8 states? Do they rail against other denominations, against lost souls? Do they say God wants you rich, ala Crefro Dollar?

This is a copy of his ministry outreach to you:

"https://www.creflodollarministries.org›Daily-Confessions

Daily Confessions | Creflo Dollar Ministries - CDM International"

"If there are areas in which you would like to see change, your tongue is a powerful tool to help bring about that transformation. The following confessions can be useful on your road to manifestation. s. monthly. Choose a one-time amount. $200. $100. $50. $25. "

This is just one of many false prophets out there. Some are blatant, some are sneaky. Beware.

Rely Upon <u>The Teacher</u>, the Holy Spirit

When I went to bible college, I was naïve. I was foolish and followed their denominational line without varying from what was taught. I did not think for myself. I did not think whether my teachers were right or wrong (by the way, why do we put a 'w' before wrong and not before right?) It actually took me years to realize that some of their teachings were not in alignment with the Bible. So, please do not make the mistake I made. Take what your teacher says and study it.

Always remember that the Holy Spirit is our Chief Teacher. We can read the Bible and learn doctrines, but only the Holy Spirit shows of the truth of the teachings, and He shows us the purpose of that truth which is:

THE GOODNESS OF GOD

I memorized Galatians 2:20 way back in bible college, *"I have been crucified with Christ; it is no longer I who live, but Christ lives in me; and the life which I now live in the flesh I live by faith in the Son of God , who loved me and gave Himself for me."* I have had that verse in my mind for over 40 years but never took the time to really dwell on it. And that is what a lot of us do. We read the verse, accept the verse and continue on. But we really don't understand; we understand enough of the verse to think we got the whole thing! But we don't.

For example, Galatians 2:20*; "I have been crucified with Christ."* Have you? How have you been crucified with Christ?

Your body? No. Your soul? Your spirit? Were you there on the cross with Jesus? So, what exactly does this mean? Only the Holy Spirit can reveal this to you. But you must do your part and think about it, and not just gloss over it.

I heard once that you only really know something when you can explain it to a child. Try it. Can you explain that you are 'the light of the world' to a child? Think about it. Here are a few other biblical ideas to think through. Let's say you are talking to a group of five-year-olds. Explain the Bible words, righteousness, sinful nature, everlasting life, etc. (By the way, this is a fun exercise for your mind and your spiritual growth!)

Allow the Holy Spirit to do His work. It is your job to meditate on the Word. If you don't do your job, you don't allow the Holy Spirit to do His work. Remember, the Holy Spirit exercises all the fruits of the Spirit, therefore, He is patient. He isn't going to force you to meditate and pray about the verses. But if you do not, you actually hinder the work of the Spirit. The Holy Spirit works with you, not against you. It is a cooperative effort. We need to listen to the Holy Spirit. After all, *"The Lord is the Spirit...."* 2 (Corinthians 3:17).

Take time to dwell on His Word. The promise Jeremiah 33:3 is great! It says, *"Call to Me, and I will answer you, and show you great and mighty things, which you do not know."*

So, what does it mean to be crucified with Christ? I can easily give the theological definition, but that is a cop-out. I don't have the complete answer, but I do have the beginning of the answer and God will surely teach my heart the full answer as I meditate over the next few months. (I wrote this months ago and still haven't taken the time to meditate on it fully. Shame on me!) ((I just took the time to meditate once more on these verses and focused on Jesus the Lord. My biggest error in thinking about these verses was thinking my actions had anything to do with this. I didn't go to the cross. It wasn't anything I did. Not by my action. But Jesus included me in His crucifixion. That gives the verse sense. And, with Him I was resurrected into a new life, a life led by the Spirit of God. Etc.)) I hope you dwell on it and seek the Lord's guidance and let Him reveal it to you. Remember, His love is so great for you. He has so much for you. Seek Him. Meditate on His Word. Allow the knowledge of His love to permeate your mind, Romans 12:2 *"And do not be conformed to this world (sinful patterns and empty lives), but be transformed by the renewing of your minds, that you may prove what is that good and acceptable and perfect will of God."*

Prayer: O Precious Lord Jesus, teach us Your Word in our hearts and not just in our heads. May your Spirit guide us into all truth as You have promised. Grant us to put away our worldly ways and religious thinking. Instead, we ask that You help us to seek You and follow You. Thank you, Jesus. Amen.

Behind God's Word

Why was the Word of God Written?

Sometimes you can love the Word of God without loving God. It's like reading a love letter and loving the letter more than the person who sent it. It's just wrong. Let's go behind the Word and look at the Writer of the Word.

Let's ask ourselves these questions: Why was the Word of God written? Why did God take the time (centuries) to write it, choose the right people from all walks of life, from a sheep keeper to a king, from a fisherman to a theologian, etc.? What was the intent behind the writings?

The first question that pops into my mind when thinking about what's behind God's Word is what kind of Person wrote it? What is He like? What is His character? Then, I ask myself why He wrote it.

To Show Us Who He Is

God is our Creator. He formed us from the dust of the ground. *"Then the Lord God formed the man out of the dust from the ground and breathed the breath of life into his nostrils, and the man became a living being."* (Genesis 2:7). He is our creator.

He is called Yahweh and Elohim. Yahweh means the Eternal One and Elohim expresses the idea of Creator and Lord of the Universe. He is the Ultimate Reality if you will. In other words, He is The Eternal and the Creator and Ruler of the universe.

The Character of the Writer

Let's start at the beginning and look for the character of the Writer. This takes us to Genesis the first book of the Bible. 'Genesis' means a giving birth, a beginning, and in this case, THE Beginning! In the first two chapters of Genesis, we find that when God creates things (like the world, the sun, moon and stars, air, land, water, vegetation, animals, and people). He uses the word 'good' to describe His Handiwork. His handiwork is completely good. There were no marrings, no defects, no need to replace or start over. Our natural world is full of beauty, grandeur, and wonder. This shows that the character of God is good and is Himself full of beauty, grandeur and wonder.

The character of God can be seen in Exodus 33:18-19 as well. Moses had asked God to show him (Moses) His glory. This is how God responded: *"And he (Moses). said, 'Please show me Your glory.' The He (God). said, 'I will make all my goodness pass before you...'"* I believe it is Bob Differbaugh who said, "The goodness of God appears to be the sum total of all of God's attributes. The goodness of God may thus be viewed as one facet of His glorious nature and character and also the overall summation of His nature and character." The often-used Chrisitan saying and response, "God is good." and "All the time." is quite true and biblical.

Character Assassination

Many don't see God that way. The devil tries to deceive us into believing that God is not good. He doesn't call God an outright liar (at first), but He does try to plant doubt in our minds, especially the minds of the lost, those who do not know

God and who lie in the lap of the wicked one like puppets on a string. The devil questions God's goodness. He did it to Eve and he does it to you and me as well.

The devil relentlessly attacks the character of God. You see this by so-called scientists who choose their scientific data based on their own prejudices, and you also see it by people who feel they are entitled to more, and by those who blame God for their hurts, etc. The devil is real and attacks the goodness of God at every turn. Another example of this is the entertainment and movie industries.

Some of the best movies ever made often seem to have a Christian hypocrite as the antagonist. Cool Hand Luke, an excellent movie, has the guy spouting Christian sayings being the most evil. The greatest war movie before 'Saving Private Ryan' was 'Zulu' a pretty-much true story. All except for the drunken missionary and his daughter who caused morale to plummet while they were with the British army. (This is completely false; the missionary and his very young daughter did no such thing. They left the area as requested.) A more modern movie, 'Shawshank Redemption' also has the leading evil guy spouting religion. The list goes on and on. These are all great movies seen by millions and all contain the subtle idea that Christians and their God are evil.

Counteracting Character Assassination

The one truth I always use again this ruse of Satan is to quote John 3:16 *"For God so loved the world that He have His only Begotten Son that whoever believes in Him should not perish but have everlasting life."* This verse shows the depth of the goodness of God no matter what is going on in my life. If God asked His only Son to come to earth and pay the price for my redemption, even though it cost Him terrible suffering and death, dying with all my sins on His pure and holy body, I know fully and completely that God is good and I am His and He is good to me. And not just to me but to everyone who calls on Him. Romans 8:32 states, *"He did not even spare His own Son, but offered Him up for us all; how will He not also with Him grant us everything?"* Since God loves us that much, surely, He is good.

So, the One behind the Word is good. His Word is good. It can be trusted because the One who created the heavens and the earth and everything in them is good.

He is not just good, He is kind. He is gentle. *"Come to Me, all of you who are weary and burdened, and I will give you rest. All of you, take up My yoke and learn from Me, because I am gentle and humble in heart, and you will find rest for yourselves."* (Matthew 11:28-29) Jesus is talking about Himself and how He treats people, how He treats you and me. When we falter, and we all do, He doesn't condemn us. He brings us back to him in a kind and gentle way. When I deserve judgement, He gives me grace. When I deserve punishment, He wraps His loving arms around me and hugs me. Character counts and His is unsurpassable.

Do you see the goodness of God? Look carefully and look deeply.

Why Write?

Now comes the next question: Why did God write His Word? I believe there are many reasons God wrote the Bible and the answers are found in His Word. Here, I will cover what I think are the most important ones.

To Show us Who We Are

God wrote His Word to show us ourselves. The God of all good states in Hebrews 4:12 *"For the Word of God is living and powerful, and sharper than any two-edged sword, piercing even to the division of soul and spirit, and of joints and marrow, and is a discerner of the thoughts and intents of the heart."* And Proverbs 21:2 states, *"Every way of a man is right in his own eyes, but the Lord weighs the hearts."* Through His Word, God gives us a true picture of ourselves. We can see that God knows our hearts, our innermost being, even more than we ourselves do. His Word, words that He wrote, are for our benefit. The Word of God is a mirror to our souls; it shows the true nature without the cosmetic thoughts we use as a silkscreen to see ourselves as good. Romans 3:17 clearly show us our own nature, *"There is no one who does what is good, not even one."* Psalm 36:1-2 add, *"There is no dread of God before his eyes, for in his own eyes he flatters himself too much to discover and hate his sin."*

God knew we were going to need His Word. That is one reason why He wrote it. To help us see the naked truth that we are not right in our hearts. He did this in order to show us our need for a Savior, one who can make us good.

To Show Us The Way Back

He also wrote His Word to show us the way back to Him. Isaiah 1:18 states, *"Come now, and let us reason together," says the Lord, "Though your sins are like scarlet, they shall be as white as snow; thought they are red like crimson, they shall be a wool."* He calls for us to reason with Him, to figure out the way back to Him and His plan for our lives.

Finally, Matthew 1:21 states, *"... you shall call His name Jesus (Savior), for He will save His people from their sins."* Matthew 1:23 shows us the true nature of Jesus Christ, *"See, the virgin will become pregnant and give birth to a son, and they will name Him Immanuel, which is translated 'God with us.'"*, God sent us a Savior, His Own Son, to bring us back to Him through the forgiveness of sin. This we could not do on our own. This is the most important reason God wrote His Word; to tell us He was sending His Son to save us from our sins!

How will You Respond?

There are many more reasons why God wrote His Words to us. It teaches us how to live, how to treat others, how to worship, etc. This should give us a better understanding of the Author of the Word and why He wrote it.

These truths about God beg the question: How are you going to respond?

You have three choices. You can follow and obey the Word of God, you can ignore the Word of God or you can twist the Word of God into something you are more comfortable with. The last two choices will keep you in your sins and send you to hell as the Word of God clearly says. The first choice brings you back to God and in fellowship with Him. Jesus Himself said, "*Repent and believe in the good news!"* (Mark 1:14).

Repent simply means 'turn back from' (your wicked ways). It means: Open your heart to God's love. Some people say that one must confess their evil deeds and then trust Christ to save them. And in some cases, this is true, but I beg to differ that it must happen in all cases. When one comes to Christ, that in itself is an act of repentance. When one opens their heart to God's calling, that is an act of repentance. They have repented and have chosen to follow Jesus.

For example, when I got saved, God simply asked me, "Do you want my love?" I had just heard the good news preached and then God revealed to me that it was all true. So, He asked, "Do you want my love?" In my heart I cried out, "Yes!" and He flooded me with His love and I was born again. I was born again in that instant without going over each of my sins or even thinking about eternal punishment.

John Wesley once said how he had been counseling a man about his soul after one of Wesley's preachings. The man got up and walked away. And Wesley saw that he got saved while walking away. The Spirit of God changed Him right then and there. Reverend Wesley said that every Christian worker should have that in their theology.

Repentance is the whole heart turning to God, which automatically then turns away from evil. Some people, many people, need this deep conviction of sin and need to prostrate themselves before God, others just fall into the loving hands of Jesus. Who does what? God knows, we don't.

You will know if you repented. If you love God and want to follow Jesus and you have the inner witness of the Holy Spirit that you are His child, you have repented and believed. Hallelujah!

If you haven't these things, even though you may be very religious, you need to turn completely to God and if led, confess your sins to Him.

(Having said that, I have repented thousands of times as a Christian. As I John 1:9 says, *"If we confess our sins, He is faithful a just to forgive us our sins and cleanse of from all unrighteousness."* I didn't really know about sin until after I got saved. Now, I see the need to repent daily as I often displease the Father. To be clear, I am not repenting for salvation, that's settled, I am repenting because my heart needs to and repentance restore my fellowship with God.)

Prayer: You, O God, are beautiful. You are good. All goodness comes from You. You wrote Your Word for us. Thank you. In Your Son's glorious Name, amen.

Trusting God's Word

Is God Trustworthy?

Can God be trusted? Can I trust Him with my hopes, my aspirations, my family, my job? These are fair questions. After all, if I am going to let Him tell me where to go and what to do, how can I be sure He knows where I should go and what I should do? Does He have my best interest at heart? This question of trusting God is of primary importance and needs to be addressed in our minds and hearts before we can truly believe God's Word.

There are several criteria with which we can test this idea of believing God's Word. First, does God know the future? Yes. Next, is God powerful enough to help us in our life? Yes. Does God have the best plan for our lives? Yes. Does God want me to have peace of mind? Yes, and yes to all of these questions of faith.

But the most important reason for trusting our God is found in Romans 8:31-32, *"What then are we to say about these things? If God is for us, who is against us? He did not even spare His own Son, but offered Him up for us all; how will He not also with Him grant us everything?"*

This does not mean life will be a bed of roses, on the contrary, followers of Christ will be persecuted. The rest of Romans Chapter 8 speaks of victory in Christ in spite of troubles and afflictions. By trusting God, we overcome the world's way of dog-eat-dog, the fleshliness of our own selfish desires and the devil's attacks on us.

The Living God is trustworthy.

Does God Promise to Take Care of Us?

The Bible says, *"You will keep him in perfect peace, Whose mind is stayed on You, Because he trusts in You. Trust in the Lord forever, For in YAH, the Lord, is everlasting strength."* Isaiah 26:3-4 NKJV

A key point in this verse is, *"Because he trusts in you."* Let's personalize His Word. Instead of the word 'he', insert your name; "Because Betty trusts in You (the Lord)." Does that make a difference in your thinking? It does mine. It encourages the reality of what God is saying. This is what God wants us to do. He wants us to personalize His Word.

If we read the Bible just for facts, even theological facts, we miss the fullness of what God intended when He wrote these Words to us. If we read the Word of God and continue on in life unchanged in our own lifestyle and way of thinking, we miss out on the blessings of God and the soul-truths that create a better inner life and a better person. For example, as I meditated on what this verse means, I had to stop and think of a few things. First, why did the Lord include the phrase 'is everlasting strength'? How does that relate to the thoughts of God in this verse? After a short meditation, I realized that it is the strength of God which we are trusting in.

He has the strength to see me through every problem, every issue, every circumstance in this life. This is great news for the mind, but do you take it in to your will? Is this merely intellectual gymnastics or do you let it sink deep into your soul? Do you trust Him to take care of you daily? You should; and so should I. And I do when I am focused on Him. As the first part of the verse says, "You will keep him (insert your name) in perfect peace, Whose (your name) mind is stayed on

You." We are not trusting in just an all-powerful god, but in the God who actually cares about us, who is for us, who really loves us. He has your back.

He has shown in many other verses that He loves us (John 3:16), and that He wants the best for us (Jeremiah 29:11), etc. If God has your back, why should you fret about things? You should live your life to the best of your ability and trust God in all things, things at work, things at home, things in your soul, things in my kids' lives, etc.

The question is: Do we believe this? This is the essence of faith. The words 'faith' and 'believe' come from the same Greek word (pistis). Faith is our will to trust God, believing are the actions we do when we are trusting God.

Believe is an action verb. It requires 'doing' something. This may seem like a trite saying but think about it for a minute. You hop in your car because you believe it will start and take you where you want to go. You turn on the living room light switch because you believe the lamp will come on. Believing something causes us to act. In the book of James it says, *"... faith, if it doesn't have works, is dead by itself."* (James 2:17)

Where is Your Believing?

Ask yourself these questions: Where is your faith placed in all situations? Knowing that God is not surprised by any situation, but always has a plan for us, are you going to believe? Are you going to act on your faith, or is it just a faith of your intellect and not of your will? When we are between a rock and a hard place, let's remember that Jesus is our Rock and that He will act according to our faith and take care of the hard place. And if we are faithless in that particular circumstance, He remains faithful (2 Timothy 2:11). He will rescue us. But we must keep in mind that when we are faithless, we lose the blessings of being faithful and our faithless actions can and do cause difficulties in our lives and others as well.

A good example of this is found in Genesis when Abram lacked faith and went down to Egypt and lied about his wife, saying she was his sister thereby implying she was not his wife. God was still faithful to deliver him; but the consequences of his actions lasted years. (Actually, it lasted centuries as the descendant of Hagar and Abram, Ishmael had himself many descendants who were always against Israel, even to this day.)

God is always faithful. The question is: Are we faithful to trust Him?

Can We Get More Faith?

If you are like me, you desire to increase your trust in God. Let us remember Romans 10:17, *"So then faith comes by hearing, and hearing by the Word of God."* As you immerse yourself in the Word of God your faith will grow. Of course, we have to act on what we read. Faith comes by reading, listening to and studying the Word of God. When we commune with God in this way, acting out our faith becomes natural, like breathing. The Word of God is God's own voice and this is the only source of unblemished, absolute and errorless Truth. God's Word has no errors, no differing philosophical points of view to consider, no maybes. *"....Indeed, let God be true and every man a liar."* (Romans 3:4). God says His Word is true. Proverbs 30:5a says, *"Every word of God is pure."* So, do we trust what He says? Do we act on what He says?

One way of looking at this is, though you don't see Jesus, you trust Him. On the other hand, you do see what He says, and you should trust that too!

Do We Live the Faith We Have?

Living by faith implies knowing that faith, knowing what we believe. Some people find the Bible difficult to understand and ask, "How do we trust God's Word when we don't understand it? After all, there are some Scriptures that I just don't understand. Some of His sayings are beyond my comprehension." And this is true for all of us.

There are different reasons for this. Maybe we haven't truly studied His Word on that point. Maybe we have just read it and listened to the pastor and haven't really thought about it. Maybe we have disobeyed in that area of our life that God has quit speaking to us about that for a season until we are ready to listen and obey.

Maybe God says that it is not the time to give you that facet of truth because there our other truths you need right now. Maybe your soul isn't ready for that truth because you are still in the baby stage of your Christian walk. And maybe you haven't obeyed the other truths God has revealed to you and He is waiting patiently for you to submit to His Way. He is waiting for you to repent. I have found all of these to be true in my life. But the one thing I do know. Psalm 119:105 *"Your Word is a lamp to my feet and a light to my path."*

We need to follow the truth we already know and let God reveal other truths to us at His timing. He will light up our path and give us the right truth at the right time.

To get more faith in action, we must use the faith we have. God builds on that faith. It's like the two fishes and five loaves of bread that fed thousands. God can and will increase our faith as we, like the Apostle Peter, begin to step out of the boat on the little faith we have. Give to God the obedience of that little faith you have and watch Him cause the increase!

The best times you have in life are when life is freaking you out. Then God can show what He's capable of for you. Then our faith is tested and when we pass the test, our faith increases. Thank God for the tough times! Sometimes, it is not easy. Jesus at the Garden of Gethsemane. He prayed hard for the cup to pass from Him, but He chose to do God's will. Let us choose the same.

Prayer: Father, when You speak through your Word, grant us a willing heart to trust you and act on what You say. As You have promised in the Psalm, guide us, be our light. In our Savior's glorious name, Jesus, we pray. Amen.

Using God's Word

Use the Verse God Gives You

Today while waiting for my dental appointment, I read and meditated on Psalm 121: *"1. I lift my eyes toward the mountains. Where will my help come from? 2. My help comes from the Lord, the Maker of heaven and earth. 3. He will not allow your foot to slip; your Protector will not slumber. 4. Indeed, the Protector of Israel does not slumber or sleep. 5. The Lord protects you; the Lord is a shelter right by your side . 6. The sun will not strike you by day or the moon by night. 7. The Lord will protect you from all harm; He will protect your life. 8. The Lord will protect your coming and going both now and forever."*

Verse seven stuck out to me. The Holy Spirit, Who dwells within each and every believer, made me think about that. *"He will protect your life."* My life! What part of my life? My physical life? After all, that's what I usually think of when He talks about my life. But then I thought: why am I limiting what God says? It doesn't say my 'physical life', but my 'life.' This must therefore include every aspect of my life! My spiritual life, my relationships, my financial life, my emotional life, etc. All of my life!

So, I started thinking about some of the emotional baggage I have that I certainly do not want. Emotional baggage is harmful to me and to those around me. The biggest thing about emotional baggage is that it can drag us down to negative feelings and thoughts, just the opposite of what God has for us. It is one of the devil's playgrounds. He knows our weakness and the thoughts in our mind are his Play-Doh. He shapes it how he wants, and it is never good. It can really hurt us. And it drains your energy from all the good that you could be doing.

So, I prayed, while in the dentist chair, "*God, why didn't you protect my emotional life as you promised?*" Immediately God answered, *"Because you never asked for My help when you got that baggage."* "Oh." I thought, "He's right. I didn't ask." So, I pointed my finger toward Heaven and said in my mind, "God, You're right."

The girl cleaning my teeth stopped cleaning and asked me what I wanted. So, I told her that I was praying while she cleaned my teeth and was just telling God that He was right. A little awkward, but a good witness, nonetheless.

But now, I have claimed that verse for protection for all matters about my life. (Claiming a verse simply means that you are going to intentionally trust for God to do what He says He will do.) And we should never forget that when claiming a verse, we should praise God with thanksgiving! This shows that we will trust Him before it ever happens.

God will protect me. God loves it when we take Him at His Word. But there is a word of caution here: We shouldn't be presumptuous. We must not use God as a vending machine where we just press the button to get what we want. We must allow the Holy Spirit to impress upon us the verses we should claim.

So, what about that baggage? Well, later I prayed and rebuked that baggage. I don't want that baggage stinking up my life. After all, we are new creations in Christ Jesus according to 2 Cor. 5:17. The devil may try to bring the baggage back into my life. My reliance on the Word of God will keep him at bay.

Philippians 4:8 is a verse that works well when we use it, *"Finally, brothers, whatever is true, whatever is honorable, whatever is just, whatever is pure, whatever is lovely, whatever is commendable - if there is any moral excellence and if there is any praise - dwell on these things."* Note the word, 'dwell'. It's not just a passing thought, but something you need to keep thinking about. It is good to dwell on the love of God and on the truths of God. After all, He is our 'dwelling' place!

There seems to me to be two ways God uses to take care of the emotional baggage, just as there are two ways God can heal. He can use a doctor-type (the natural way), or He can heal directly (the supernatural way), by His touch. I believe this is the same with emotional baggage, and any other thing in life. Anyway, I did pray, and I did rebuke the baggage and could sense the power of God taking so much away!

The Devil's Army

I truly believe that most of that baggage was the devil's army of demons attacking me through false bondage. A pastor friend once told me that it's like a man in a jail cell who keeps pounding on the steel bars to get out, not realizing that the door is unlocked and all he has to do is push it open.

Often the devil's demons impress negative thoughts and attitudes on us and tell us that is who we are. But God commanded us in I Peter *5:8 "Be sober, be vigilant; because your adversary the devil walks about like a roaring lion, seeking whom he may devour."* We must be vigilant because the devil is against you, hates you and hates your family. He will do all he can to destroy you. We must remember that we are God's children. We have a new nature, the Holy Spirit dwells within us. He cleanses us, He guides us, He teaches us all about who we are. He tells us to be vigilant!

Use the Word for A Transformed Mind

We Christians need to transform our minds according to Romans 12:2, *"Do not be conformed to this age, but be transformed by the renewing of your mind, so that you may discern what is the good, pleasing, and perfect will of God."* This is how we can better follow God's will for us. The Word of God assists us in this transformation that God calls for.

Transformation of the mind is necessary because we have been trained to think as the world thinks, selfishly. We can be cruel and selfish or we can be nice and selfish, but selfish, nonetheless. Jesus, Himself, said in Matthew 7:11 that, "you who are evil, know how to give good gifts to your children." Jesus said we are evil. So how does that affect our 'goodness'?

Our goodness is what we choose to do because it suits our personal interest, not necessarily because it is good. A murderer can be nice. After all he doesn't murder everyone, only those he wants to. A man in business can be very cruel to those around him, as long as he doesn't get called out for it (he fears peer pressure). A religious zealot can say kind words of encouragement to many, but inside he may well be arrogant and spiteful. He hates sinners and condemns them. Jesus, on the other hand, hates sin but died for those sinners. Transformation of the mind means thinking as God would have us to think as He thinks, and not as selfish man thinks.

In the very next verse in Matthew, Jesus said, *"So, whatever you wish that others would do to you, do also to them."* Matthew 7:12(ESV). This is not normal to our way of thinking. We might think of these words as niceties, but not real, just platitudes. We usually are quick to forgive ourselves when we fail to "do unto others" and chalk it up to being human.

But Jesus was not joking when He said these things. We all know the way of the world only too well. Now we must learn the way of God. This calls for a change in our thinking, a transforming of our mind. The Word is God is a key tool that helps us to be transformed in our thinking and to be closer to imitating Christ and His thinking.

Use the Word to Clean Up Your Mess

And let us not forget that since God loves us so much that He sent His Son, Jesus the Messiah, to come and die for our sins, He is not going to leave us hanging in the lurch now that we are His children! He will certainly clean up the mess that sin made in our lives, especially in our souls. Matthew 11:28-29 says, *"Come to Me, all you who labor and are heavy laden, and I will give you rest. Take My yoke upon you and learn from Me, for I am gentle and lowly in heart, and you will find rest for your souls."* NKJV. Jesus is talking about rest in the here and now, not the hereafter. Our souls can rest in Him. God can restore relationships, failures, and anything else that we messed up. It may take much on our part, but God will fix things or give us the grace to accept things that He chooses not to fix at this time.

I once heard a testimony from a young man who wanted to kill a family, any family. He had a terrible childhood with a father who had left and his mother entertained various men who never took notice of him. He said, while giving his testimony in a small Alabama church, he wanted to line up a family and shoot the youngest one first, and then the next in line, etc. But, thank God, he got saved and God changed his heart. He became a mild-mannered, happily married man and if he hadn't given his testimony, one would have never guessed his past. That is what God does for those who come to Him: rest for the soul.

Healing

God uses His Word to bring healing, whether physical, mental, or emotional. Matthew 6:33 states, *"But seek ye first the kingdom of God and His righteousness and all these things will be added unto you."* All what things? All the things you need for abundant life here and now, just as Jesus promised us in John 10:10, *"A thief comes only to steal and to kill and to destroy. I have come so that they may have life and have it in abundance."* Yes, we are called to have the 'abundant life'. A full and good life. Seek His Kingdom first and He will take care of you. 'Seeking His Kingdom first' is the key.

This does not mean a carefree life. There may be times when God calls us to suffer for His Name. Romans 8:36 says, *"As it is written: Because of You we are being put to death all day long; we are counted as sheep to be slaughtered."* At that time of our suffering, I firmly believe that God will give us peace and comfort as we trust Him. We need to remember that we are to give ourselves to God as a living sacrifice (Romans 12:1) *"Therefore, brothers, by the mercies of God, I urge you to present your bodies as a living sacrifice holy and pleasing to God; this is your spiritual worship."* Think of Peter in jail. He had the peace that passes all understanding while in jail. The guy was fast asleep! The angel of the Lord had to roust him out of there! And the disciples who were beaten with rods had joy! They rejoiced that they were allowed to suffer for the name of Jesus.

Use the Word as a Guide

"Your word is a lamp for my feet and a light on my path." (Psalm 119:105). God's Word guides our life. It guides our life with principles for living such as *"Love your neighbor as yourself."* (Mark12:31), *"Carry one another's burdens..."* Galatians 6:2), etc. This is not just how we should live, but which paths in life we should take as well. Proverbs 3:5-6 states, *"Trust in the Lord with all your heart and lean not on your own understanding. In all your ways acknowledge Him and He shall direct your paths."* KJV

When we have specific questions about the choices we make in life, God often uses situations, people and circumstances to steer us in the right direction. And sometimes even an angel! I distinctly remember on time when I was jogging St. Vincent Island, on the Florida panhandle, just west of Little St. George Island. I was told that the island had a whole lot of snakes and that scientists would come to study the snakes there. I had arranged for a boat to pick me up at the end of the island after my jog and get me back to my van.

As I was jogging, I came to a point where a tree had fallen across the narrow beach and was half in the water. Thinking about all those snakes on the island, I froze. Both the path behind the tree and the one in the water around the tree looked dicey. I didn't know what to do. But then I felt my shoulders being turned toward the water path. I was like someone was standing behind me grabbing my shoulders to point me in the right direction. So, I went in that direction and was soon at the end of the island when the boat showed up. Something like that ever happen to you? I've heard firsthand accounts about these sorts of things happening. The Bible does say we have guardian angels (cf. Matthew 18:10 and Hebrews 1:14).

God will show us in His Word what we need and what we have as His children if we take the time to meditate on what He reveals to us. Thus, we don't just read the Word of God, but we use the Word of God as God intends. The next time God impresses upon you some passage in the Bible, take time to meditate on it. As it says in Psalm 1:2, *"But his delight is in the law of the LORD, And in His law he meditates day and night."* Biblical meditation means to think about it. And God says to think about it fully, even all day and all night.

Use the Word to Help Each Other

Every Christian has a mission. The basic mission of each of us is to love God, and encourage and help others and enjoy fellowship! *"Therefore encourage one another and build each other up, just as in fact you are doing"*(1 Thessalonians 5:11).

"The precepts of the Lord are right, giving joy to the heart." (Psalm 19:8).

"For you were once darkness, but now you are light in the Lord. Live as children of light." (Ephesians 5:8).

"For whatever was written in the past was written for our instruction, so that we may have hope through endurance and

through the encouragement from the Scriptures." Romans 15:4

As blood flows through our veins giving nutrients to the body, so the Word of God flows through the veins of our souls nourishing us with the best God has to offer. And this isn't just for our own edification, but this enables us to help each other in the body of Christ and to bring others into His body.

Just as Christ shared His life with us, we too, are to share our lives with others. After all, the Apostle Paul says, *"we who are many are one body in Christ and individually members of one another."* (Romans 12:5) We are to build up each other, encourage each other, enjoy each other. Throughout the Gospels, Jesus instructs us to do what is right. Much of His teachings involve helping others. The story of the Good Samaritan found in the Gospel of Luke very clearly shows this.

Some guy was beat up, robbed, stripped naked and left for dead. The religious leaders who walked by the poor fellow forgot what they were supposed to be religious about! The Levite and the priest, symbols of God leadership in Israel, failed miserably to follow God's plan. They just passed by. The Samaritan, who the Jews despised so much that they wouldn't even talk to them, helped the guy. We are to be the good Samaritan.

When Jesus said, *"Love your neighbor as yourself,"* (Matthew 22:39), what does that mean to you? This love isn't a feel-good moment, but a commitment to wanting the best for your neighbor.

How to do this? Well, since Jesus did it, we need to read the Gospels and see how Jesus did it. He certainly wasn't maudlin over the woe-is-me people, nor did He play to their 'poor-me' attitude. But He loved them. Let us learn from the Gospels how God loves people and, as God's true children, let us do the same.

Use God's Word to Encourage Each Other

Some years ago, my aunt was sent to a hospice in a town near me. She was lucid with an alert mind. She had become a believer late in life and loved the Lord. One day I went to see her. I wanted to share a couple of verses with her. One of the verses I have since forgotten but the other was John 14:1-3, *"Your heart must not be troubled. Believe in God, believe also in Me. In My Father's house are many dwelling places; if not, I would have told you. I am going away to prepare a place for you. If I go away and prepare a place for you, I will come back and receive you to Myself, so that where I am you may be also."*

When I got to the hospice center, I asked the office attendant if I could make copies of the two verses so they could be enlarged and easily read by my aunt. They allowed me to enlarge them and when I went to see her, I showed her those verses which were large enough to put on her wall. She exclaimed that she was looking for those verses to read but couldn't find them. She was overjoyed to read them.

God had put those particular verses in my heart to get them to her because He wanted to encourage her for the journey ahead. I was able to be a blessing to her with those verses!

God has a habit of doing this in people's lives. Someone will share a verse from God's Word with you and it will be just what you needed in your spirit. It will comfort and fortify you. God uses us to encourage others.

Remember those times in your life that God has used someone to give you His Word. Remember how that helped you through your difficulty? Sometimes it's a friend that gives you a word which the Spirit uses to strengthen you and put a pep in your spiritual step again. Sometimes, it is your spouse, or the preacher or a complete stranger. God uses us to encourage each other.

"This is my comfort in my affliction. Your promise has given me life" (Psalm 119:50).

"Therefore encourage one another and build each other up as you are already doing" (I Thessalonians 5:11).

"And let us be concerned about one another in order to promote love and good works, not staying away from our worship meetings, as some habitually do, but encourage each other, and all the more as you see the day drawing near" (Hebrews 10:24-25). *"Speaking to one another in psalms, hymns, and spiritual songs, singing and making music from your heart to the Lord"* (Ephesians 5:19).

"No foul language is to come from your mouth, but only what is good for building up someone in need, so that it gives grace to those who hear" (Ephesians 4:29).

"Based on the gift each one has received, use it to serve others, as good managers of the varied grace of God" (I Peter 4:10).

We can see that God wants us to encourage each other, to help each other, to encourage each other to be of good cheer as we look together to the author and finisher of our faith.

Let me give you one last story of how the Word of God is used to encourage us. It was around 1990 and I had just recently returned to the Lord after a 10-year hiatus. The Lord was so gracious and surrounded me with His love as I bowed on bended knee and sought Him. But the months that followed were quite difficult. In fact, I was struggling most of the time and in despair a lot as well. The devil was severely attacking me.

I remember one night listening to Warren Weirsbe on Back to the Bible radio, and I was suffering much in my soul. Brother Weirsbe stopped his program, said that there was someone out there that needed this particular verse, and he quoted the verse at least five times. Each time he said the verse, I felt a wave wash over me and at the end of his quoting, I was free from that despair. Thank God brother Weirsbe heeded the Spirit's voice and interrupted his broadcast!

God will move mountains to help you. He often uses your brothers and sisters in Christ. After all we are the hands, feet and mouth of Jesus now. We are part of His body, doing His work. Let us use the Word of God to encourage each other.

Prayer: Father, Loving God, thank You for Your Word which reveals Your will for us and Your love for us. Thank You that we are called Your children! You gave us Jesus' own righteousness, as Isaiah 54:17 says, *"Their righteousness is from Me, says the Lord."* In His righteousness and in His holiness, we come before you and humbly ask that you grant us insight on how to use Your word, how to truly believe Your Word and to help each other so that we can please You and glorify You. Through Jesus, our Savior and Friend and Brother, we ask. Amen.

Memorizing God's Word

Our Duty and Privilege

"I have treasured Your Word in my heart so that I may not sin against You." (Psalm 119:11). In Psalm 119 verse 105 we read, *"Your Word is a lamp for my feet and a light on my path."* It is recorded that Jesus quoted Scriptures 78 times. The way He used it was in general conversation and speeches. This shows that He was very familiar with the Word of God. He had memorized Scripture. If our Lord memorized and used the Word of God so much, shouldn't we do the same?

Almost a half century ago, in Bible college, I had to memorize one to four verses for each class. Some of the verses I memorized I have used throughout my life as sure guides from God. In fact, just yesterday I memorized James 3:13. And I am considered old (according to all those young whippersnappers - lol). If an old man can do it, so can you.

As Christians, we all have a desire to be more like Jesus, to be conformed to His image. In Romans 12:2 it says, *"Do not be conformed to this age, but be transformed by the renewing of your mind, so that you may discern what is the good, pleasing, and perfect will of God."* How does this ongoing transformation take place? By the renewing of your mind.

And how does that take place? By putting the Word of God in your mind and heart and letting the Spirit of God change you more and more to God's ways. His goal for us is to be conformed to the image of Christ (Romans 8:29). Christians used to be called 'followers of the Way.' This means early Christians conducted their live is such a way as to reflect the teaching of Jesus. They lived out the image of Christ in their lives. Is this your goal as well? If so, this means we must know the Word of God and what it means. It is our duty to memorize the Scriptures.

This is what we use to fight with

When Paul spoke about fighting the devil and the armor of God in the book of Ephesians, the only offensive weapon we had was the Sword of the Spirit, the Word of God. So, unless you want to keep playing defense and let the devil keep bashing you around like a puck in an air hockey game, you need to use the Word of God. If you don't know the Word of God, it's like going into battle without a rifle: you keep getting shot at and shot up but can't shoot back.

Memorizing simply means sticking it in your brain so it stays there. Once you are thinking about it, God will use it to change you for the better.

Memorizing takes time, but it is time well spent. In our too-busy society, we need to stop and make time to meditate on the things of God. We need to take time to hide God's Word in our heart. *"I have treasured Your word in my heart, so that I may not sin against You."* (Psalm 119:11)

We all have the ability to memorize. It's exactly like a muscle; the more you use it the stronger it gets. Start with one push up. The next day do two. Before you know it, you are doing 20 pushups easily! So, start with one verse, try one verse every week, then two verses a week, etc. It is truly amazing what you will be able to do. And it is truly amazing how God will bless you in your work! It gives Him joy when we dwell on

His Word. He will show you amazing and awesome things, things that will bless your soul more than you can even dream!

Commit your memorizing to the glory of the Lord and see what happens!

Which Method Works Best for You?

How do you get started? There are different ways to memorize and you will find the one that works best for you.

Some can learn by hearing it over and over. Others have to write it down several times. Others must see it or speak it.

For me, I read it a few times, studying its meaning and when I feel almost ready, I write it down. Then I close the Bible and write it down without looking. I then check my work and fix the errors that always come up. Then I write it again making sure to correct those errors. I do this until I can write it and say it three times in a row without any mistakes. And sometime during that day I recite it again. The next day as well. Then I have it memorized. That's my way. Your way will probably be different. You can use the following ideas to find the ideal way for you to put the Word of God in your mind. Because if it is not in your mind, it won't be in your heart:

You can read it out loud. Please read and understand the context first as verses taken by themselves with no contextual understanding leads to many errors in understanding the Bible.

Here are some ways that people memorize scripture. Find the one that works for you:

You can put it to music or rap it.

You can write it several times or put it on flash cards.

You can build word pictures in your mind.

You can listen to it as you fall asleep.

You can discover your own unique way of memorizing scripture!

It takes practice and the more you practice the better you get. Build that memory muscle! Find the way that works best for you and practice, practice, practice.

Obey, and Fight to Win!

What are the benefits of memorizing God's Word? Much in many ways! First, we obey God by hiding His Word in our hearts. Secondly, we won't get deceived like Eve and Adam.

The devil wants to trip us up in our walk with the Lord. He tried to trip up Jesus several times. He did trip up Peter many times. He'll throw Scripture at us either changing some words, like He did to Jesus, or using the Word of God out of context. Taking the Word of God out of context is bad theology and bad theology ruins lives. You and I have seen this over and over. A false teacher preaches at a church and people are led astray and fall into all kinds of problems. I have seen false teachers mess up individuals lives so badly that the family broke up and the poor fellow ended up in jail. These new 'prophets' are a danger to Christians. Sad, very sad. Handling the Word of God accurately in our hearts prevents this and keeps our walk with the Lord pure and on the right path.

Memorizing His Word Deepens our Devotional Life

Another benefit is that we can pray the Word of God back to God. We can bless God by trusting His Word and claiming His promises. Jesus questioned if there would be faith when He returned (Luke 18:8). By using the Word of God in our prayers we remain faithful. We can call upon God to remind Him of what He said. God expects this of us. It's not that we need to remind God as He certainly doesn't forget things. But we show God that we are trusting His promises in His Word. It shows Him that we trust what He says. It is faith in action. It's believing God's Word.

How often have I used Proverbs 3:5-6! *"Trust in the Lord with all your heart, and do not rely on your own understanding; think about Him in all your ways, and He will guide you on the right paths."* I've used these verses hundreds of times! When I do, my outlook almost immediately changes to one of trust and peace. I quit worrying and start trusting. After all, since Jesus died for me, He surely will keep me going! *"He did not even spar His own Son, but offered Him up for us all; how will He not also with Him grant us everything?"* (Romans 8:32). I recite the words, letting God know I am trusting His Sayings and thanking Him for it! Faith thanks God before the promise is fulfilled.

Purity

Another thing is purity. We can keep ourselves pure by memorizing the Word of God. Simon Peter said in II Peter 1:2-8, *"May grace and peace be multiplied to you through the knowledge of God and of Jesus our Lord. His divine power has given us everything required for life and godliness through the* ***knowledge*** *of Him who called us by His own glory and* *goodness. By these He has given us very great and precious promises, so that through them you may share in the divine nature, escaping the corruption that is in the world because of evil desires. For this very reason, make every effort to supplement your faith with goodness, goodness with knowledge, knowledge with self-control, self-control with endurance, endurance with godliness, godliness with brotherly affection, and brotherly affection with love. For if these qualities are yours and are increasing, they will keep you from being useless or unfruitful in the knowledge of our Lord Jesus Christ."*

All of this flows through the knowledge of Him. It comes from reading and living the Word of God. A godly life follows the Word of God. Purity matters to God. It should matter to us as well. Again, *"I have treasured Your Word in my heart so that I might not sin against You."* (Psalm 119:11).

Let's Make God Happy!

There is one more reason for memorizing the Word of God. It pleases God. We make our Father happy when we memorize His Word. The Psalmist says, *"How sweet are your words to my taste, sweeter than honey to my mouth."* (Psalm 119:103). Also, Proverbs 2:1,5 *"My son, if you accept my words and store up my commands within you, then you will understand the fear of the Lord and discover the knowledge of God."* Proverbs 4:5 says, *"Get wisdom, get understanding; do not forget my words or turn away from them."* And finally, Proverbs 7:1 says, *"My son, keep my words and store up my commands within you."* This makes it very clear that God wants us to 'store up' His Word within us, in our minds and hearts. You and I have the power to make God happy. Let's make God happy!

Joy!

I must add one more reason: Memorizing God's Word gives us joy! Jeremiah, often called the weeping prophet, says in Jeremiah 15:16, *"When your words came, I ate them; they were my joy and my heart's delight, for I bear your name, Lord God Almighty."* We Christians have joy when we memorize God's Word. It is in our nature (our new nature) to enjoy the Word of God. I remember when I was watching a friend's house for a day or two. It was in the country. The wi-fi was out and there was no TV or internet. So, finally, after realizing there was nothing to watch, I decided to open the Bible. But this was not first on my list. In fact, I opened it grudgingly. But I had a great and amazing time reading First Corinthians! God had to take those other things away to get to me. It became a wonderful couple of days.

Find the way to memorize that works best for you. Practice. Strengthen your memory muscles. Put God's Word in your mind and hearts. Fill yourself with God's Word. Do this and you will have purity, joy and wisdom. May the love of God overflow our hearts as we obey His Word.

Prayer: Wonderful Father, grant us the privilege and pleasure of memorizing Your Words. Your Words are from You and they are precious. Open our hearts to see this. In Jesus' Name, amen.

Doing God's Word

Our Works Show God's Glory

In the Book of James it says, *"be doers of the Word, and not hearers only, deceiving yourselves."* (James 1:22). James also says, *"faith by itself, if it does not have works, is dead."* (James 2:17).

James is talking to the church. To you and me. There are so many theologians who say works aren't necessary to get you to Heaven. And that is very true. Only the blood of Jesus for the forgiveness of sin gets anyone to Heaven. But what they don't say is that the works you do reveal your faith. No works? No faith. Jesus was very clear about this. In Matthew 5:16, Jesus said, *"Let your light shine that they* ***may see your good works*** *and glorify your Father in Heaven."* Or, as Rich Mullins, that amazing Christian songwriter said, "Faith without works is like a screen door on a submarine."

For the Christian, good works is a testament to the new birth, the new heart that God has given him in Christ. Ephesians 2:8-10 says, *"For by grace you have been saved through faith, and that not of yourselves; it is the gift of God, not of works, lest anyone should boast. For we are His workmanship created in Christ Jesus for good works, which God prepared beforehand that we should walk in them."* We should walk, i.e., live our lives, in the good works that God has already prepared for us. In this sense, we are predestined to good works.

So, how do we know what good works God wants us to do? That is a very good question. It's like the question, "Okay, I'm saved; what now Lord?" I am not an expert in this, but I can tell your how God has led me to do good works in my life.

God called me to be a preacher one Monday evening while I was traveling from Ohio to North Carolina. In those days, I normally prayed for an hour every Monday evening from 7 to 8 p.m. Well, it was getting to be about 7:00 p.m. But since I was taking a long journey and liked to put the miles behind me, I told the Lord that if I saw a church in the next five minutes, I would stop and pray for an hour, otherwise, it wasn't His will to pray on that particular Monday evening. I saw a modern brick country church on my right with a very nice entranceway and benches outside so I stopped to pray. As I was praying, God asked me if I would be willing to become a preacher. I thought about it and decided that, yes, I would become a preacher as God requested. After the hour ended, I went on my way.

But it doesn't stop there. I had no idea of how to become a preacher. (Notice that God did not say pastor, but preacher.) I am qualified to preach and teach, but I do not have a pastor's heart. Pastors are truly special.

When I got back from my trip, I attended a country Pentecostal church whose preacher was a wonderful, old-time preacher with wisdom and grace. In his sermon Brother Adams mentioned that we should 'bloom' where we are planted. So, I just continued to do what I was doing, witnessing, speaking when the opportunity arose and teaching and discipling. The key was to bloom where God put me. It is no accident where God has put you. It's time to bloom!

Follow God's Leading

My friends thought I should become a pastor and urged me to submit my resume to various church in the area. I was hesitant as I wanted to wait on the Lord, but I decided after several months to go ahead and see if God was in their words. In the end, nothing came of it. Good! It was not the right track for me according to God's will.

Then I went on a vacation my daughter designed, a week in Punta Cana, Dominican Republic. It was a wonderful vacation with my daughter, her husband, my son and his girlfriend and me. One morning I was beside the pool, reclining in an oversized recliner and I just lifted my hands to Heaven and praised God. Suddenly I saw a word in the sky with letters in flaming white. The word was "Write" Hmmm.... Now what? (Ever notice that these things happen almost always when we are praising God?)

I didn't know what to write. So, I just started writing things. But then I found an old book full of prayers written in 19th century writing style. The prayers were beautiful, but the language was archaic. I decided to rewrite the book, add some chapters on prayer, delete and add some other prayers and the outcome is ***'Yesterday's Prayers for Today's Christian.'*** And I have written various articles and tracts, etc. that I hope please our Jesus and bless the folks. For me, this is doing God's Word, along with loving God and my neighbor. A good thing would be to ask God what works He has prepared for you.

Bear Fruit

The fruits of the Spirit compel us to do God's Word. Love, the first fruit of the Spirit, is an action word, not just a feeling word. If we love someone, we will do what is best for them. Think of your spouse, your children, etc. We Christians should have it in our hearts to want the best for every single person we come across. Sometimes we are in a position to help those who want help. And we should. But we need to help with wisdom. Giving a couple of bucks to a druggie on the street is not wise. Asking him if you can pray for him and his family is wise.

Good works are natural to the true believer. We naturally help people. It could be as simple as opening a door for someone or as complicated as taking care of your sick neighbor. This is helping people, people that God created and loves.

If we have joy, we will automatically encourage others to acquire that same joy. If we have peace, we will show that peace to others and they too will know that there is a peace that is beyond all understanding.

Jesus said, *"You will know them by their fruits."* (Matthew 7:16). Therefore, we can conclude from Jesus' remarks that doing equals evidence, i.e., fruit. Fruit grows from a tree. Fruit is the natural item that comes from within the tree. So, it is with Christians. Fruit is the natural outcome of who you are. So, how is your fruit? The fruit of the Spirit comes from the Spirit. We enjoy the Spirit's fruit of love, joy, peace, etc. We, in turn, are to share that fruit with those around us. This is the Spirit of Christ reaching out to a world He loves. He is using you and me. Therefore, let's not let Jesus down. Let's share His fruit. After all, He certainly shared His fruit with us!

Recently I have been reading the Sermon on the Mount in Matthew chapters 5 - 7 almost daily. I still need to read it more to fully understand it. At the end of His beautiful sermon, Jesus said, *"But everyone who hears these sayings of Mine, and does not do them, will be like a foolish man who built his house on the sand."* (Matthew 7:26). Let us therefore show forth our fruit by doing God's Word. Let us build our house on the Rock and not on the sands of self-deception.

Prayer: Father of mighty works, Creator of all we see and don't see, work in our hearts to do Your works here on earth. Your works are to love You and love each other; to love people so much we share the Good News of your Son's sacrifice for them. In the name of Your Glorious Son, amen.

Living God's Word

The Word of God is Living, Use it to Live

Tonight, as I was editing a paper on God's promises, I ran across a verse that affected me. It was John 14:27 *"Peace I leave with you, My peace I give to you; not as the world gives do I give to you. Let not your heart be troubled, neither let it be afraid."* The phrase 'neither let it be afraid' stood out to me. From long experience I knew that the Holy Spirit was giving this word to me. I could sense it. (John Bunyan in his famous autobiography often talks about the work of the Holy Spirit impressing God's Word on us. It is a spiritual feeling that usually lightens the soul.) But this time, instead of just thinking about it for a few seconds and letting the thoughts of the verse slip by, I decided to really mediate on it.

Upon meditating on this phrase, I thought that God was telling me something was causing me fear and that I should figure out what it was and tell my heart to stop being afraid. After all, a Christian should not walk around with a shroud of fear masked by a fake smile, or to be like one who is quickly offended.

Jesus told us to let not our hearts be afraid (John 4:1, 27). This means that fear is a choice. Fear is an emotion. Emotions come from thoughts. According to Lazarus and Lazarus in their book, 'Passion and Reason: making sense of our emotions,' emotional arousal stems from your thoughts on a particular situation. Is the situation for or against your goal? Is it going to help you or harm you? The situation in one sense doesn't matter. What matters is how you appraise it.

In Hamlet, Shakespear said, *"For there is neither good or bad but thinking makes it so."* (Hamlet, Act II Scene 2) Fear stems from thoughts of possible harm to someone or something we care about. We can control this fear according to our Creator.

In his excellent book, FEAR: The Good, the Bad, and the Ugly, R.T. Kendall explains the three types of fear. There is the good fear, i.e. the fear of God; the bad fear, the fear we have because we do not trust God; and the ugly fear which is devil induced. The fear I am talking about here is the bad fear.

How Should We Then Live

As a Christian, we should live God's Word by appraising our lives according to Scripture. We should realize as we follow Christ, that *"... all things work together for the good of those who love God; those who are called according to His purpose."* Now that's positive thinking!

Our minds need to be renewed. How can I live God's Word when I live in fear?

Our Past is Part of Us

We all have things in the past that affect us, some of them we know and some we do not know. The things we don't know we say live in the realm of our subconscious. There is precedent for this: Romans 8:26 says, *"In the same way the Spirit also joins to help in our weakness, because we do not know what to pray for as we should, the Spirit Himself intercedes for us with unspoken groanings."* We really don't know how to pray at times. We don't have such a clear picture of the workings of our soul as God does. And these issues can affect how we live the Christian life.

Time to Grow

When one gets saved, God gives that individual New Life, and the indwelling of the Holy Spirit. But God does not just zap their emotional state. He doesn't wipe the hard drive of our mind and emotions. Our 'history' is still there and needs to be dealt with. He brings joy and peace, etc., but He doesn't usually fix the past issues of the soul or psych. He does makes everything new in our life. He gives us love, joy and peace and the knowledge of forgiveness of sins.

It's like a newborn baby entering the world. The baby is kept warm, fed, hugged, etc. But as the baby grows, he has to struggle to roll over, pick up his head, walk, etc. In the same way, the Christian has to begin to grow and take control of his life according to the Word of God. Can God fix the soul? Yes! Does He just zap it? Sometimes. Not usually. Why not? I think He wants us to come to terms with the past hurts and work through them to forgive and ask forgiveness and to set our minds aright as it says in Romans 12:1-2. *"...Be ye transformed by the renewing of your minds."*

This often means the emotional triggers that afflict the Christians have to be dealt with. Those past emotional scars have to have the scabs ripped off that old wound. It must be opened and dealt with. We can't just hide them behind our words of affirmation. It doesn't work that way. We are just suppressing our emotions, which then will make it even worse! It's like putting a band aid on gangrene. It is just going to get smellier and more infected.

As His children, we need to deal with the past in an intelligent and godly way. I personally have experienced this in my life at different times and the healing of dealing with the past lightens the soul and makes me a more true and effective Christian. I remember years ago, someone asked me, "Who hurt you?" I had no idea of what they were talking about because it had been pushed out of my thinking for so long. But it seemed obvious to them. And, unbeknownst to me, that hurt deeply affected my relationships with others. That comment was made when I was in my 20s. I finally found out what it was and dealt with it when I was in my 40s.

Some of us have been unloved, we have been molested, we have been abandoned, rejected, neglected, etc. And just as the body needs healing from physical ailments and wounds, so too our emotions need healing as well.

It is imperative not to mask our emotional needs by waving the Christian flag. This is fake and people see it. The emotions will only stick their ugly faces out later in an even worse manner. We need to positively deal with those past hurts. We need to take them to the cross.

Stunted Growth

Some Christians think this is hogwash. But their lives show their insecurities. They keep praying and say they trust the Lord, but still worry about things in life. They still don't have that true comfort of presence and peace that God has for them. I know Christians who always pray but are always worried.

People have fears. Even Job had fears and said as much in the oft-forgotten verse, Job 3:25, which says, *"For the thing I feared has overtaken me, and what I dreaded has happened to me."* Why did God pick on Job? I think it was to cleanse him of this fear. (Lest we boast about not having that fear let us remember that that was the only thing Job had against the will of God. I certainly can't say that!)

Freedom from the Past

I see so many deep sorrows that Christians have, even though they love the Lord and have a true desire to please Him and to serve Him. They think they shouldn't have these emotional triggers and problems so they cover them up by more devotion, more 'work for the Lord.' This can be a pretense of devotion in order to cover up their pain which they think should not be there. After all, 'I am a Christian.' they think and, 'This should not be happening to me.' And the thoughts can get much worse.

Emotional Slavery

How to be free from the enslavement of these emotions?

We need to seek God's guidance as He assists us in dealing with the past, so that our soul can be set free and healed. Jesus wants to give us complete rest for our souls. He often uses good, thoughtful people in our lives to help us.

First, acknowledge that you indeed have these emotional trigger points that aren't supposed to be there.

Second, ask God for wisdom in dealing with them. He will give you the avenue to freedom. After all, He has promised to 'give us our daily bread'.

Third, when you get an emotional upheaval, think, and keep thinking why that exists in you. Ask God to reveal the cause of that emotional upheaval. Get to the bottom of it. For me, it almost always goes back to my childhood or youth. And when I can pinpoint that event, I can reason out why I feel that way and then take corrective actions.

In fact, just last night I had an emotional moment. I was dancing with a friend at a social dance and she pulled me aside while we were dancing. This is common if we are going to run into another couple and the lead (me) doesn't see it. But I asked her why and she said the pro dancer was walking his dance partner to the floor. Immediately I bristled. "Who does this guy think he is?" I asked myself. "I don't need to move for him. He is not even dancing yet. He can get out of my way!" I said as much to her and she looked at me strangely. Shortly after, I then thanked her for getting us out of the way. My ego was bruised, and maybe rightly so, but grace is a better way to go. So, I have to fix that in order to be a good witness to those around me. Was I being a little insecure? Maybe.

Finally, we need to resolve the underlying issue. It may well be you need to forgive someone(s). Or you may need to realize that nothing was your fault and you couldn't stop it, (whatever it is) from happening. Or it may be that you need to understand that the reason behind the emotional trauma is false.

One of the hardest persons to forgive is yourself. For example, a man in his 40s in Sunday School in a church on the east coast of Florida told the class of his abusive father. The abuse was directed more often than not tooward his mother. The fellow at Sunday School had been a good Christian for a long time, but still had this pain in his heart, a guilt.

I asked him if he forgave his dad and his mom. He answered in the affirmative, so I asked him if he forgave himself. At that, he abruptly got up with tears in his eyes and walked out of the class. In his mind as an adult, he thought he failed for not stopping his father. But as a young child, he didn't have the understanding or power to step in, as he later thought he should have had to stop the beatings. So, he blamed himself. Once he realized this, he could forgive himself, for in fact he had done nothing wrong. He had carried this guilt for years, not knowing it was based on faulty reasoning. Finally, he could forgive himself. He came back into class before it was over and I think it helped him resolve the emotional pain he kept inside.

Act on His Promises

Then, turn to Jesus and claim His promises. Claiming a promise is simply telling God that His Word is true and trustworthy. Let's use Proverbs 3:5-6 as an example, *"Trust in the Lord with all your heart, and do not rely on your own understanding; think about Him in all your ways, and He will guide you on the right paths."* Situations come up in life that are hard, scary and difficult. They can create physical, emotional and spiritual turmoil. So, I have to remember this promise from God to guide me and all will work out. I quote this verse, I pray this verse and I trust this verse. God has never failed me. Not once!

Therefore, if God says He gave me His peace, then I should claim it and say thank you. Now, that fear may come back, but then again, we turn to Jesus and 'look full into His wonderful face.'

Trust God

Look at it this way, if you told someone you were going to help them work on their house tomorrow and they said, "I am not sure you will.", or "How do I know you will?", what would you think? You would think that this fellow doesn't trust you! He thinks that you are not a man of your word, that you might be a liar! Well, that is exactly what we are telling God when we don't take Him at His Word. This is why we should act on His promises. The Hebrews were in the desert for 40 years, but it could have been just one year. The reason they were there so long is that they doubted God's Word.

Sometimes, I feel like I am still in the desert. Remember that God did indeed take care of them in the desert, but He kept them there because they didn't trust Him. He had to teach them to trust Him before they could be strong enough to enter Canaan. How could He help them if they didn't trust Him? He couldn't! So, am I in the desert? Am I trusting Him completely as I should? Am I fulfilling God's plan for my life? Or am I like the Hebrews, looking at the problem and not at the God, the God of solutions? And I must consider the question of whether I am in God's will. We must ask Jesus, our Shepherd, to reveal to us where we stand on trusting Him.

The biggest and most awesome adventures you will have in this life is stepping out on faith and following Jesus. Just ask Peter, the only other guy who walked on water! Remember, He is in control, and He has told you not to fear.

Prayer: Father of mercy, grace and peace, grant us wisdom and obedience to live Your Word and so glorify Christ in our lives. Amen.

Breathing God's Word

Fresh Air for a Needy Soul

Have you ever heard the expression, 'a breath of fresh air', or, 'breathing down one's neck', or like Saul, before he became the apostle Paul, he was 'breathing out threats'? We Christians should be breathing God's Word. Breathing God's Word means to be so full of His Word that it just naturally breathes out of you. The Word of God has become so much a part of you that it naturally comes out whenever you interact with folks. Let's remind ourselves how Jesus interacted with people.

The first surprise is that tax collectors and 'sinners' loved to hear Jesus speak. *"While He was reclining at the table in the house, many tax collectors and sinners came as guests to eat, they were reclining at the table with Jesus and His disciples."* (Matthew 9:10). Why do these kinds of folks love to hear Jesus speak? What made Jesus so special?

I think the following verses will help us understand why people loved to listen to Jesus. *"A good tree doesn't produce bad fruit; on the other hand, a bad tree doesn't produce good fruit. For each tree is known by its own fruit. Figs aren't gathered from thornbushes, or grapes picked from a bramble bush. A good man produces good out of the good storeroom of his heart. An evil man produces evil out of the evil storeroom, <u>for his mouth speaks from the overflow of the heart."</u>* (Luke 6:43-45).

Jesus' tree is the best fruit tree there has ever been! People want that fruit! Jesus spoke out of the overflow of His heart. He exemplified grace and truth. Look at what Jesus told His disciples! *"Jesus called them over and said to them, "You know that those who are regarded as rulers of the Gentiles dominate them, and their men of high positions exercise power over them. But it must not be like that among you. On the contrary, whoever wants to become great among you must be your servant, and whoever wants to be first among you must be a slave to all. For even the Son of Man did not come to be served, but to serve, and to give His life a ransom for many."* (Mark 10:42-45). Jesus, who was full of grace and truth, had a servant's heart.

Do You Have a Servant's Heart?

Jesus had a servant's heart toward everybody, not just his friends or followers. He was approachable. He wanted to help even the vilest of persons. He breathed God's Word. Jesus, God Himself, showed us how to breath God's Word. He lived it (and still does) and He wants us to live it, too.

Jesus used the Word of God extensively. He declared freedom to the captives, woes to the faithless, and called those who were beaten down and burdened to come to Him to find rest. (Isaiah 61:1; Matthew 11:21-22; Matthew 11:28-30). He was steeped in the Word of God. He knew its value and therefore used it extensively. As the Psalmist said in Psalm 1, He meditated on the Word night and day. In II Timothy it says the Word is 'God-breathed' and Jesus breathed that Word to all.

Jesus loves people, all people. He showed compassion and grace and mercy to all. Psalm 145:8-9 says, *"The Lord is gracious and compassionate. Slow to anger and great in faithful love. The Lord is good to everyone: His compassion rests on all He has made."* And Mark 6:34, *"So as He stepped ashore, He saw a huge crown and had compassion on them, because they were like sheep without a shepherd. Then He began to teach them many things."*

Jesus was full of 'grace and truth'. (John 1:17). He did not just feel sorry for folks. He helped them in life and helped them understand life. He did it with grace. But in His grace, He did not hide or obfuscate the truth.

An Australian evangelist and his teenage son stayed with us while we lived in Korea. He told me that he used to preach the word through the windows of the pubs. One time a pub patron slammed the window to shut the evangelist up. Seconds later another pub patron opened the window back up because he wanted to hear the words of life.

Tell the Whole Truth of God with Grace

Jesus loved people so much He told them the truth. Even if it killed Him! In His great love for the rich young ruler (Mark 10:21), He told him to sell all and follow Him. Jesus knew what was keeping this young man from following Jesus and He told him. The young ruler went away shocked and sad because he was rich! Hopefully, he decided to follow Jesus after the resurrection. Jesus did not hide the truth of the cost of following Him. So, in our compassion and love, we must give the truth of God.

So many Christians have a feel-good type of servanthood, but grace and truth must stay together. Many folks are nice to a fault. They do not want to hurt people's feelings so they don't speak the truth. They just act nice. In a very real sense, they will sacrifice that person to hell in order not to make them feel bad now. How insane is that? They get a good feeling from feeding the homeless, but they stop there. They don't give the truth. They don't tell them how to come to God. They don't want to offend the folks. That is a very foreign idea to Jesus.

Compassion without truth can be emotional nonsense that doesn't help anyone, it just makes the so-called compassionate one feel better. When someone gives some money to a street person, the giver feels so good about doing the 'right thing'. The street person, on the other hand, now has money for another drink or some meth. This is compassion without truth.

True compassion speaks for itself. For example, a lady I know made a meal for a mom that had just had a baby. There was no preaching involved but that act of compassion was a connection which showed the mother she really cared about her. The time for sharing the love of Christ would come as the Spirit leads. This is godly compassion.

Truth must accompany compassion. I've seen truth without compassion on the streets and on TV. I can't stand the preacher with an angry look on his face yelling the truth. It's like taking good food and throwing it at the starving person. The folks who do this are often smug and arrogant and detestable in God's sight. Some Christians do this, and sad to say, I used to be one of them. But God cut my heart one day and took that blight off my soul. Praise God!

If we do not put forth the truth of sin, salvation and Jesus, we are not showing compassion and love for those around us, we are just pleasing and placating their feelings and our own feelings. Let's speak the truth in love (Ephesians 4:15). We need, in our helping people, the mindset of presenting the whole truth with love. We, like Jesus, need to be full of grace and truth.

Be Filled With the Holy Spirit

Another facet of breathing God's Word means to be filled with the Holy Spirit, the author of God's Word. It means letting the Spirit of God use the Word in your life, your thoughts and your conversations. Many Christians read God's

Word, but not many live God's Word. What about you? Do you meditate on the Word? Do you ask God for insight when you don't understand? He will give it to you. Do we ask God for wisdom in dealing with people. Do we ask God to put love in our hearts for all those around us? God will do it. He is amazingly patient and kind.

We can see when someone is filled with the Spirit because that person exhibits the fruits of the Spirit. These are the ones who have love, joy peace, showing forth compassion and truth working together.

Let us breath the Word of God. Just like the air we breathe. When we breathe the air, we don't usually recognize that we are doing it, but we are. It is natural. Let the Word of God become natural in your life.

Prayer: O Most Merciful God, grant us to be merciful too. Grant us to love as You love, with great compassion, wisdom and truth. Fill us with your Holy Spirit and lead us accordingly. To the glory of Jesus we pray. Amen.

Revealing of God's Word

"I still have many things to tell you, but you can't bear them now. When the Spirit of truth comes, He will guide you into all truth. For He will not speak on His own, but He will speak whatever He hears. He will also declare to you what is to come. He will glorify Me, because He will take from what is Mine and declare it to you." (John 16:12-14)

How God Reveals His Word

Before I became a true Christian, the Bible was a strange book. When I was around ten or eleven, I was hanging out in my room and was curious about the meaning of life (That's not exactly how I put it back then). So I picked up a pocket New Testament and opened it up. It opened to the book of I Corinthians and I started reading. After a few minutes of reading, I put it down thinking, "There is nothing here about life. In fact, I haven't a clue what the books says!" So, I put it back and never looked at it again in my childhood. It just didn't have anything for me.

Ten years later, at the age of 20, a couple of friends knocked on my door one Sunday morning. And they kept knocking. Finally, I got out of bed, went downstairs and opened the door. Rick Frey and Mike Cooper were there and they wanted me to go to church with them. Now, Rick and Mike were not known to go be church goers. I couldn't figure out what was going on so I told them I didn't want to go to church. (Church to me was getting all dressed up, meeting old folks you don't really know, singing some slow songs and listening to some guy who often read from a book and didn't really say anything of importance at all.) But Rick and Mike said the place was in a guy's basement just down the street and that I didn't have to get dressed up.

So, I went. There were a bunch of kids around my age there. The preacher, an evangelist, was a stocky guy of about 40. It was his house. He preached the gospel about how Jesus died for my sins and rose again, and if we asked Him, He would save us. He also mentioned that before he got saved, he was a bad guy and supported his family through stealing for three years prior to his conversion. In fact, he said, the last time he was in jail, it was for trying to kill a guy. And now here he is talking about Jesus.

I really didn't care. The message was soon over and I was ready to go back home. But first they held hands and prayed. Well, I was in the group so I held hands too. That's when God gave me a vision of Jesus on the cross, dead. God spoke very clearly to my soul. He said, "This is all true." Then He asked me, "Do you want my love?" My soul had been wanting love all my life, so I shouted in my heart, "Yes!" At that moment, God came into my soul. Everything was different. I had peace and everything around me looked the same, yet new. I had no idea what happened and later I was sitting on a kitchen chair upstairs after the service still trying to figure out what happened, some were kind of laughing at me in a friendly way. They told me that I just got saved. I had no idea what that meant.

That was the beginning of my Christian life. Unbeknownst to me, my brother and his wife, who were new Christians, had been praying for me for several months. Prayer works!

The church folks told me to start reading the Bible. So, at night after my second shift job, I went home, got out the family bible and a big dictionary. I started in Gensis chapter 1. Night after night I read the bible with the dictionary open. When I got into Leviticus I got really confused. “What does this have to do with my new life?” I asked.

Back in church, people saw my confusion and asked me about it. I told them what I was reading and they told me to start in the gospels. I did. And did God ever speak to me! I think I highlighted half the verses in Matthew chapters 5 to 7. God was revealing His ways to me through His word. After that, I started reading the Bible and God kept speaking to me personally through the scriptures, especially the four gospels. I know it was God, and His revealing the scriptures to me amazed me and my life was changed in beautiful ways I had not known to be possible.

That was over 50 years ago. But just the other day I complained to God, “Why don’t you teach psychology in your Word? (I was going through some personal issues and didn’t know what to do.)

Well, as soon as I finished my prayer of complaint, God said to me in my spirit, “Love your neighbor.” Wow! My soul was released from the angst I felt and I was free when I focused on loving the person and wanting the best for him. That is rather good psychology, isn’t it? That ever happen to you?

It happens to me once in a while, especially when I sincerely ask God about something. (One time I asked God why we have all the mentally challenged folks and why didn’t He just fix them. A few weeks later He spoke to me spirit, saying, “It’s not your business as to why, I want you to love them.” And in that moment and since then, I have always had a deep love for the mentally challenged.) It is very cool when God speaks to our hearts and the change in our attitude and emotions is often instantaneous.

You are of Royal Blood

"But you are a chosen generation, a royal priesthood, a holy nation...." I Peter 2:9.

One day at a Christian meeting, a person prayed and mentioned in his prayer about us being of royal blood. The Spirit of God revealed to my heart the truth of this verse. He let me know that I am God's child and no matter what, God will take care of me. I am a King's kid.

It doesn't make me proud or haughty, but it does give me the utmost confidence no matter who I am with or what is going on, I know that my God, my King, is taking care of his royal son and that He can be called upon any time. He watches over His royal kids. Christians are royalty in the Kingdom of God. Jesus said that His kingdom is not of this world. Yet, as He was in this world for a time, we also are in this world for a time. They did not recognize Him and they do not recognize us. But in our kingdom, the Eternal Kingdom, we are indeed royalty.

I Peter 2:9 says you and I are royalty. You and I have royal blood in us. You and I have royal blood in our veins, our spiritual veins. So, it is not just that we are loved completely and are God's children, but we all have His pedigree, His royal ring is on our finger. He has given us His royal robe of righteousness and everything that goes with His righteousness, including His pedigree! I knew this before in my mind, but when the Holy Spirit taught me, it permeated my soul. That's the revelation of God's Word to the human soul. How cool is that!

The Revelation of Fatherhood

Just think how a king treats His kids. He watches over them closely. He makes sure they are well taken care of. Nothing is too good for them and he keeps them very safe. This is the way of God's children. It is embedded in our soul. I don't have to think this when I walk around that I am the King's kid, I already know it. It is not something that I have to believe, it is who I am. This is how the Holy Spirit teaches us. Not philosophy, nor human wisdom, but truth embedded in our souls.

It is hard to put into words the revealing of God to us. But it is real. It is a spiritual truth that we need to be open to and seek. We need to seek God's light through meditation on His Word. Instead of watching the news with its negative, fighting back and forth commentaries, or TV shows that go directly against God's laws, we need to study the Word, Of course, TV is not bad it itself. How we use it can be good or bad. (I watch a lot of TV, and I like it. In olden times, people used to sit around the campfire and tell stories. TV has taken place of the campfires, that's all.)

But how can God reveal His truth to us when we are immersed in worldly matters that often contradict God at every turn? Our spiritual eyes must be focused. We just need to have discernment. If a particular movie or show is affecting us and our Christian walk, we should not watch it. On the other hand, I believe it was Augustine who said, "Love God and do what you want." I like his idea of Christian freedom. If we love God, we will love others, and not want to sin. In other words, let's not become pharisaic about life.

How much time do you, dear reader, spend studying and thinking about what God says? About His ways? About what He has done for you? About His heart? About what He wants you to do for Him? If you are like me, it is daily, but it is not enough. But let's make sure we give time to God each day. It could be while we are driving to work, or waiting for the elevator, or on lunch break. Let's think about God. And see what truths He wants to reveal to us if we just prepare our hearts and minds to receive them.

Do you every think, "What makes God happy?"

The Holy Spirit is eager to teach us God's ways. He is just waiting for the opportunity. It says in James 4:8, *"Draw near to God, and He will draw near to you..."*. This idea of getting close to God so He can help us is throughout the bible. Deuteronomy 30:1-3; 2 Chronicles 6; 2 Chronicles 7:14; 2 Chronicles 30:0; Hosea 12:6; Jeremiah 24:4-7; Isaiah 54:7. Hebrews 12:1-2 states, *"Therefore, since we also have such a large could of witnesses surrounding us, let us lay aside every weight and the sin that so easily ensnares us ... keeping our eyes on Jesus..."* If your desire is to know more about God and His ways, now you know how to do it. Clean your heart by confessing all sins, give God some of your time, and read the Word. And ask questions!

My prayer is that God will open the eyes of your heart and that God will give you the spirit of wisdom and revelation. That in the knowledge of Him, we may know the greatness of His power to us, the riches of His inheritance we have and the hope He gave. (Paraphrase of Ephesians 1:17-19). And that we will not limit God to what we know but be open to what He wants to show us. We are God's, His family, let us trust Him.

Prayer: Heavenly Father, help us take the time to seek your face and instill in us the truths of your Word, write them on our hearts and let us rejoice evermore in You. In Jesus' name, Who gave us the Holy Spirit, amen.

Honoring God's Word

The Way to Honor God

An old Korean friend of mine from thirty years ago taught me a valuable lesson. He was a Christian elder in the Korean church I attended for several years while living in Korea. He was in his eighties when I knew him. He was healthy, sharp and had been an excellent Christian elder for many years. He even stood in front of the church one Sunday and recited the entire chapter of John 14. In English! In his eighties!

We were talking one day, and he was telling me about how some years ago he loaned a lot of money to a friend, around $5000. His friend never paid him back. Years went by and he never got paid back. I asked him why he didn't go ask for his money back. He told me that the Bible says to loan money that way. He would honor God's Word instead. Well, years later his daughter was getting married, and he needed $5000 for the wedding; money he didn't have. He prayed and worried some, I guess, but, lo and behold, his friend finally paid him back the money he borrowed, and it covered the cost of the wedding! He honored God by honoring His Word. And God honored him for his faithfulness.

Psalm 138:2 states, *"... You have magnified Your word above all Your name."* (NKJV). God holds His word in very high esteem, even above His name! We should do the same. Jesus Himself said in John 10:35, *"... the Scripture cannot be broken..."* So, we can take it to heart that God's Word, His promises, His judgements, His mercy, etc. will never change. It doesn't change with cultures, countries, or over time. It doesn't evolve. It has been true and steadfast ever since God wrote it.

So, how are we to honor God? By honoring His Word. Just like my friend in Korea did. By obeying His Words even when it is tough. Even when it seems counter-intuitive. Even when it scares you.

God says, *"It is better take refuge in the Lord than to trust in princes."* (Psalm 118:9). and the prophet Jeremiah says it in much starker terms, *"Thus says the Lord, 'Cursed is the man who trusts in man and makes flesh his strength, whose heart turns away from the Lord.'"* (Jeremiah 17:5).

Did you catch that? If we trust in man, and not God, our hearts have turned away from the Lord. Many times in Israel's history the kings turned to other countries to help and each time God chastised them for it. God indeed uses men, but it is God we should trust, not man.

When God Says Something, He Means it

We are to honor God's word by trusting what is written. After all, consider the Source.

Now, it is easy to follow God's Word when it is convenient, when things are going along well enough. It's easy to be nice to your friendly neighbor, give to a charity out of your excess. But when it is difficult or it goes against our grain to follow God's Word, then it becomes a trial, a burden. And sometimes we fail. But there are ways to help us not fail.

Jesus, our Lord, showed us how to honor God's Word by quoting it and using it daily in His life, He relied on it completely. When Jesus said He was going to be resurrected, He trusted the Promise from the Father that He would raise it up again. Jesus trusted God's Word.

Jesus said the two greatest commandments in the Law given to Moses were *"Love the Lord your God with all your heart and with all your soul and with all your mind. This is the first and greatest commandment. And the second is like it: 'Love your neighbor as yourself.''* (Matthew 22:37-39). Jesus did that. We should too. Let's honor God's Word by doing what it says; let's love God and love our neighbors.

Think back to when you were a child and your mom or dad told you not to cross the street when playing outside. You did not cross the street, did you? You honored their word. And when you got married, you promised to love, cherish and be faithful to your spouse. You honor your own words when you follow them. And when someone dies and leaves a last will and testament, the court requires you to honor those last words.

Well, think of Jesus' last will and testament. In the book of Matthew, we find His last words on earth, His orders for us to follow. *"And Jesus came and spoke to them, saying, 'All authority has been given to Me in heaven and on earth. Go, therefore and make disciples of all nations, baptizing them in the name of the Father and of the Son and of the Holy Spirit, teaching them to observe all things that I have commanded you, and lo, I am with you always, even to the end of the age.' Amen."* (Matthew 28:18-20).

If you really want to honor Jesus our Lord, then obey His Words. Go make disciples. Tell others about God's gift, His only Son. And when you bring people to Jesus, show them the Words of God and the love of God. This honors Jesus' Words. Are you willing to take the time and be used by God to bring others into His kingdom? Are you just a hearer of the Words of Jesus, or a hearer and a doer of His Words?

Prayer: Loving Father, help me to trust you always, in every situation. Grant me the faith to honor Your Word. In Jesus name, amen.

(Dis)Honoring God's Word

How We Dishonor God

When we don't rest in the promises of God, this shows we don't truly trust God and what He has said. This is dishonoring God. The question is: Do we honor God or dishonor God?

Jesus said, *"When the Son of Man comes, will He really find faith on this earth?"* (Luke 18:8). It has always struck me as strange that Jesus didn't say, "Will He find love?" Or "Will He find Christians?" No, He said will He find faith. This shows the priority that our Lord puts on faith. Therefore, it seems to me that a lack of faith dishonors God and God's Word.

Our lack of faith comes from the many wiles of the devil and from our own hearts. A lack of faith in God's goodness ended Eden when Eve enjoyed the forbidden fruit. She thought God was holding back in the good stuff in life, even though she had a perfect life. She wanted in some way to be like God. Lucifer tried to be like God as well. It didn't turn out very well for him and his judgement is sure. Adam dishonored God's Words by elevating the gift (Eve) above the Giver (God). He preferred to disobey God in order to make his wife happy.

But let's not blame Adam and Eve too strongly. If it had been Bob and Betty or you or me, the same thing would have happened. And today, you and I still make those same choices that Adam and Eve made, don't we? This goes to show what a lack of faith does. A lack of faith leads us into self-glorifying sin.

Fear of Circumstances Dishonors God

One way we dishonor God is fear. We fear that if we follow God, it won't turn out well. We are scared to follow God. We see this in finances, in relationships, in all aspects of our life. How many times have we fudged in finances or not tithed as we ought or not given as we thought we were led by the Holy Spirit to give (I.e., Ananias and Sapphira)? How often have we listened to others and not to God, or not even godly counsel, because we feared the outcome?

In Genesis chapter twelve, Abram (later Abraham). went to Egypt and asked his wife to lie for him. He feared the Egyptians would kill him for his wife. He had this fear even though God had told him that he would have a son. And since he hadn't yet a son, he was not going to die yet. So, Abram's fear was completely unfounded.

Sometimes we fear a possible future failure as Job said he did, *"For the thing I feared has overtaken me, and what I dreaded has happened to me."* (Job 3:25). We fear the future.

Even the disciples showed fear. In the boat in the storm Jesus had to admonish them, *"Why are you fearful, you of little faith?"* (Mathew 5:26). Peter, that great Apostle of Christ, had issues with fear a few times. At the trial of Jesus, Peter got scared enough to lie about knowing Jesus (Mark 14:66-72). and later when Peter visited the gentile believes in Galatia, he again feared the other 'religious' Jewish believers and stood condemned by his sin (Galatians 2:11-14). And Peter was a better Christian than I'll ever be!

Let us strive to increase our faith so that when the next storm of life comes our way, we trust God, which is the opposite of fear. Let's keep our eyes focused on Jesus, the author and finisher of our faith (Hebrews 12:2). God has proven Himself so many times to each of us. Let us remember those times when the devil tempts us with the fear that God can't or won't protect us. Psalm 23:4 says, *"Even though I go through the valley of the shadow of death, I fear no danger, for You are with me; Your rod and Your staff - they comfort me."*

Fear of Man Dishonors God

We often dishonor God's Word because we fear man and not God. The Israelites feared man and thereby despised God's command in Numbers chapter fourteen when the reports came back about the land of Canaan. They even wanted to stone Joshua and Caleb for encouraging them to follow God and go take the land! As Numbers 14:11 says they feared man and rebelled against God. In their lack of trust in God they despised His command. But Jesus said, *"Do not be afraid of those to kill the body but cannot kill the soul. Instead, fear the one who is able to destroy both soul and body in hell."* (Mathew 10:28). Which brings us to the fear of God.

Fearing God Honors Him

The fear of God is a fear of the One who is in authority over you. When you were young, you feared your parents. Your mom and dad love you, but when you did wrong as a child, the threat of a spanking loomed large in your thoughts! And when a policeman pulls you over for speeding, your heart races a bit and you wonder if you are going to get a ticket or just a warning. We fear those who have power over our lives. Some call it a healthy respect for authority, like the sailors who have a healthy respect for the waters of the ocean. We don't fear God because He is evil; He is not. We fear God because He has the ultimate authority over us. To fear God is to understand that He has full and final authority over us. We all should have a very, very healthy respect for God. The Bible also says we are to 'bless the Lord'. In other words, bow down before Him and praise Him for His goodness. This implies trust. In this sense we should fear God and not be as the Israelites in Numbers chapter fourteen who feared man and despised God. God is God and man is man; let's not confuse the two.

Isaiah 8:13-14a sums this up best. *"You are to regard only the Lord of Hosts as holy. Only He should be feared; only He should be held in awe. He will be your sanctuary* (a sacred, indestructible protective shelter for those who fear and trust Him)*."* We are under God's authority and we should trust Him. He alone will save us. How He does it is His business.

So, we see that fear is one way we dishonor God. Another way we dishonor God is our own unbelief. The Bible shows that Jesus marveled at only two things. Belief and unbelief! He marveled at the centurion's belief (Mathew 8:10). and at the Jew's unbelief (Mark 6:6). Which one honored God?

Despising God

The works Jesus could not do in Nazareth would have been amazing, and no one saw them. They despised Jesus and showed this by belittling Him. "He's just a local kid from down the street." they said, "He ain't nothing." That's what they believed and spoke. So, the miracles that could have taken place didn't.

And some people simply don't want to obey God so they reject God and His Word. John 3:19-20 states, *"This, then, is the judgment: The light has come into the world, and people loved darkness rather than the light because their deeds were evil. For everyone who practices wicked things hates the light and avoids it, so that his deeds may not be exposed."* So, some people dishonor God's Word and reject its authority because they want to do their own thing. Their deeds are evil. They do not want to follow God.

Here is another example of despising God. God told the Israelites in Malachi chapter one, that they have 'despised God's name.' *"How,"* they asked. He replied, *"By offering defiled food on My altar."* He goes on to say that they are presenting God with blind, lame and sick animals for the sacrifice and keeping the best for themselves. They put their desires above God. This dishonors God. If we are not giving God our very best, we, too, are dishonoring God.

The truth is all of us are guilty of each of these ways of dishonoring God's Word. Like Peter, we all have feared man rather than God, and like Paul, we all despised the One who spoke God's Word and like King David, we all have done wicked things. But the mark of the Christian is that we have repented of our deeds done in darkness and we have put our faith in Christ and we honor His Word. We no longer fear what man can do to us because God is our shelter in times of storms, whether man-made or God-ordained. We now honor God's Word.

Dear reader, if you are not honoring God now, turn to Him, ask Him to forgive you and cleanse your heart. Decide this day to fear the Lord, to honor Him. Show God you love Him.

Prayer: Holy Father, worthy to be honored, worthy to be feared, bless us with an understanding heart of how great, how magnificent You are. To the glory of Christ we pray, amen.

Stewardship of God's Word

Protect Your Resource

There is an old ecclesiastical (church) definition of stewardship: 'responsible use of resources in the service of God'. This means that the things God gave us, we must use wisely. God gave us His Word. It is our responsibility to take care of His Word, use it rightly, and make sure it is in its proper place in our world, in our community and in our homes. This is good stewardship.

In today's society, for the most part, the Word of God is neglected. Christians are not using it as a lamp unto their feet or a light unto their path (Psalm 119:105). Some Christians in our society do not hold the Bible in high enough reverence to use it daily. Some of us seem just to use it for Christmas and Easter, weddings and funerals.

And society in general has banished the Bible from their minds and even from schools. Some countries have banished the Bible from their borders! The Voice of the Martyrs listed 52 countries where the Bible is difficult or dangerous to obtain. It is either illegal or highly restricted.

In 1962 the U.S. government took the Bible out of schools and banned school prayer. We have seen coaches and school officials fired for praying in schools or quoting scripture in the classroom. Walter Tutka, a regular substitute teacher got fired for giving an inquisitive student a Bible in New Jersey. A teacher friend of mine was told she could not pray for the kids in school.

The most important document ever put in man's hands has been shunted aside, the treasures of life and how to live life have been put on the shelf, the very words of God are considered useless or quaint. This is what the world does with God.

This is not the stewardship of His Word that God intended. So, what should Christians do?

Use It With Respect

We Christian's, on the other hand, must be the light bearers of the Word. We must be careful not to treat it as Israel sometimes treated it. When King Josiah of Judah had the temple of Israel repaired and they were in the process of making repairs, someone found God's Word and reported this discovery to those in charge.

They had lost the Word of God! This wasn't the stewardship God had planned! Fortunately, King Josiah understood the seriousness of the situation and got the leaders involved and assembled the people and read the entire law to them and made them pledge to obey the Word of God. (II Chronicles 34). It isn't very good stewardship when a whole nation loses the Word of God! We, on the other hand, have the Word of God all over the place, several versions at home, on one's phone, computer, the big screen in church. But have we too become bad stewards of God' Word? Have we lost the Word in our everyday lives? Even though it seems to be all around us, and do we use it as God intended?

Use It Responsibly

This resource God has graciously given us must be used responsibly. There ought to be a caution sticker on all Bibles: 'Caution: must be used with love and compassion, otherwise results will be negligible and sometimes negative!" Sometimes we Christians throw a verse at some 'infidel' thinking that will shut him up and win the argument! I have been guilty of this more than I care to admit. How about you? Is this how God wants us to use His Word? Is this good stewardship of God's Word?

We Christians sometimes forget that His Word can be counted on more than anything else in this universe! Jesus quoted it verbatim to stop attacks of the devil (Matthew 4), then He used it to show people that God loves them and how to return to God. He also used the Word of God to warn people of the reality of judgement and hell (Matthew 10:28; Matthew 23:33; Luke 12:5). How He said those words were just as important as Him saying those words. So, let's take a quick look at Jesus' attitude when He used it.

Use It the Right Way

First, Jesus is humble and gentle. He helps people find rest for their souls (Matthew 11:29). According to Matthew 12:20, he does not hurt those who are hurting, *"A bruised reed shall he not break, and smoking flax shall he not quench..."*. After all, Jesus came to save us, not to condemn us *"For God did not send His Son into the world that He might condemn the world, but that the world might be saved through Him."*

Jesus did speak harshly when necessary, as seen in Matthew 11:20-24, *"The He proceed to denounce the towns where most of His miracles were done, because they did not repent; 'Woe to you, Chorazin! Woe to you, Bethsaida! For if the miracles that were done in you had been done in Tyre and Sidon, they would have repented in sackcloth and ashes long ago! But I tell you, it will be more tolerable for Tyre and Sidon on the day of judgement than for you. And you, Capernaum, will you be exalted in heaven? You will go down to Hades. For if the miracles that were done in you had been done in Sodom, it would have remained until today. But I tell you, it will be more tolerable for the land of Sodom on the day of judgement than for you.'"* So, we see that Jesus, in His wisdom, spoke the right way to the people He was addressing. To those sin laden and crushed by this life, He gave hope; to those who would not repent He pronounced judgement.

We see that Jesus used the Word of God with wisdom, truth, humility and grace. Those who needed comfort He comforted; those who needed chiding, He chided; to those were so calloused against God, they needed to know they were in even more danger than Sodom and Gomorrah. May you and I pray for wisdom to speak the Word of God in a godly manner, humbly, and truthfully. This is the proper stewardship of God's Word.

Use It as Intended

To be trustworthy stewards of the Word of God we must use it as God intended.

As Jeremiah recorded, we must eat (internalize). God's Word, *"Your Words were found, and I ate them. You Words became a delight to me, and the joy of my heart!"* Jeremiah 15:16. And Jesus said, quoting Deuteronomy 8:3, *"Man must not live by bread alone but on every word that comes from the mouth of God."* (Matthew 4:4). The Word of God is our manna from Heaven. As mentioned earlier, when Israel spent those 40 years in the desert, there was scarcely any food so He provided them food from Heaven, manna. They ate this for 40 years. They gathered it daily, a double portion on Friday to prepare for the Sabbath.

The Word of God is our manna. This world is a desert of spiritual life. We must gather the Word of God daily and chew it and swallow it, letting it go into the innermost recesses of our soul so it can feed our hearts and minds. We shouldn't just read it, we need to chew on it, to think about it and how it relates to our situation, our lives. Then we need to allow it to do its work in us by obeying it. The Word of God is *"alive and sharper than any two-edged sword, able to discern the thoughts and intents of the heart."* (Hebrews 4:12). The apostle Peter says in I Peter 2:2-3a, *"Like newborn infants, desire the pure spiritual milk, so that you may grow by it for your salvation, since you have tasted that the Lord is good."* We must desire His Word in our hearts for our spiritual health. We must be devoted to the Word every day. This is God's plan for us. This is good stewardship.

So, we Christians must follow our Master in holding high God's Word. We must put God's Word ahead of man's ideas. In the proper stewardship of God's Word, we must use it for ourselves and share it with others.

We must be clearly against sin and have compassion for the sinner. We must use it to encourage our brothers and sisters. This takes prayer, wisdom, and study.

God's Word puts the heart of God into the soul of man.

Prayer: Heavenly Father, thank you for your Word. It is precious to us. Please grant that we be good stewards of your treasure. In our Lord's Name, amen.

Spend Time With God's Word

"Your words were found and I ate them. Your words became a delight to me and the joy of my heart." (Jeremiah 15:16). *"Your decrees are my delight and my counselors."* (Psalm 119:24). *"Your Word is completely pure, and Your servant loves it."* (Psalm 119:140).

When you love someone, you want to spend time with them. It really doesn't matter what you are doing, just being together is wonderful. When you love God, you want to spend time with Him as well. This is done by prayer, and reading and studying God's Word.

The Word of God is indescribably good! It is not just a love letter from God; it is not just a self-revelation from God; it is not just a book of instruction from God. It includes all these things, but it is much, much more. It is a treasure chest full of precious gems, gold and silver.

The more you spend time in God's Word, and obey it, the more of these beautiful gems of life God reveals to you.

Do you love to study the Bible? I do. I love to study the Bible and talk with others who love to study the Bible as well. It is so rich in meaning. There are so many varied ways to study. I can study languages, etymology, archaeology, grammar, history, contextual and cultural ideas, etc. In fact, I have an over-abundance of study materials just for studying the Bible.

No matter whether you have a morning devotional you like to ready or a bunch of study materials, spending time with

God in His Word is food for the soul, encouragement for the heart and luminous for the mind.

Loving the Word Means Following the Word

But I must make sure that I obey the Bible while I study the Bible, and I pray for the Holy Spirit's teaching to my mind and heart when I study also. But sometimes I forget the purpose of studying the Word of God. I forget that it is to love God with all my hearts mind, soul and strength and to love our neighbors as myself (Matthew 22:33-40). I forget to follow the Word.

I used to be a great debater on the Word of God. If some brother or sister had a different opinion about theological topics, such as eternal security, dispensationalism, I would make my points and counter points strongly. Unfortunately, this was often said without love. Fortunately, God showed me the error of my ways and now I still like to discuss or debate the Bible, but it is done in love and doesn't usually escalate to a back-and-forth debate. I am by no means perfect, but I have come to realize that people I differ with really do love the Lord and most theological issues take second place to that. Otherwise, I would still be a scribe or a Pharisee!

Our Life Must Reflect the Word of God

Some of the most amazing scholars throughout history have been the most loving people. Alfred, Pusey, Chrysostom, etc. It is said of Henry Alford, that great Greek scholar and a man of many achievements, "Privately as well as publicly his gentle winning sympathy was ready to be offered to each one who sought it, whether in joy or sorrow." And even after he 'retired' from being the spiritual guide of the congregation, he spent the afternoons visiting the poor inhabitants of his district.

E.B. Pusey, a Christian scholar and a great mind, who knew several languages well, a professor at Oxford University, was known as kind, warmhearted and sincere. Disregarding his own safety, he personally served the sick during the cholera epidemic of 1866 and devoted much of his energy to helping the poor.

Chrysostom, whose scholarly work on the New Testament is still read today, over 1500 hundred years after his death, was such a kind leader of the church in Constantinople that when the king and queen sent their guards to arrest him because he called them out on their evil doings, throngs of people surrounded the church and those sent to arrest him couldn't get in the building!

It amazes me, much to my short-sighted thinking, that these and many other scholars of the Word of God were the most intelligent and kindest of men. These men were not just hearers of the Word but doers as well.

What about you and me? Do we spread kindness wherever we go? Are we devoted to helping others as God directs? Is our soul happy? Do we show it? (Yes, sometimes we are tested by God to increase our faith, but most of the time we should exhibit the fruits of the Spirit so others may partake of that fruit.)

Love the Author

So, it is good to study God's Word, but we must not get caught up in the Word without the love for the Writer of the Word. The study of the Word of God, called theology, is beautiful if we study it to understand God and His ways more clearly and obey Him more fully. If we don't study God's Word to obey it, we become arrogant with our knowledge and mean-spirited to those who disagree with our theology. We become cold to life around us. Theology without love for God and our fellow man is an insidious evil destroying the very things God is building, His church, His Kingdom.

The difference between knowing God's Word and loving God's Word was shown to me at a Wednesday night bible study in a little town in Alabama when I was traveling through heading back to Ohio from Florida. It was a Sunday and I wanted to stop at a church for a service. I always like to go to new churches when I travel. Some are amazingly wonderful.

Well, this particular church had a Bible study and there was about ten of us. One of the men, about 30 years old, was eager to share the gospel with the world. His countenance was happy and you could see his desire to share the Word. Another man, twice as old, kept shooting down the other's ideas and exuberance. And he did it by quoting and explaining Scripture. He controlled the meeting with arrogant speech while quoting the Bible.

It was so evident and so clear who loved God and who loved self. One loved the Author of the Word and one loved himself and used the Word to lord it over others. Just like the Pharisees in Jesus' day. Just like some church leaders today.

We must be careful not to be too enamored in our own denomination's theology. Remember that the scribes and Pharisees were also steeped in their own theology. But Jesus showed them the difference. He said, *"but I know you - that you have no love for God within you."* (John 5:42) Therefore, let's make sure that in our theological pet peeves we do not forget to love our brothers as ourselves. I fellowship with believers in all denominations. I have Catholics brothers and sisters whom I love to fellowship with. Baptist, Pentecostals, Reformed, Methodist, Seventh Day Adventist, etc. Denominations are not a barrier to those who love Jesus. When Jesus prayed that we be one (John 17:21), this was not a denominational unity but a spiritual unity.

If You Love God, You Love His Word

Those who truly love God, love His Words as well. Jesus is the perfect example of this. He quoted the Word of God often. He explained the Word of God and put His stamp of authority on the sureness of the Word of God. Some of our Lord's greatest teaching comes from explaining the Word of God. One just has to read the Gospels to see how saturated Jesus was with the Word. Jesus is even called the Word of God. He embodies the logic, the reasoning and the purpose of God. After all, He is God. Sometimes we should read the Bible as if Jesus is sitting right there with us; because He is.

Yes, we need to love the Word of God and cherish it and think on it. The Spirit of God heals us, refreshes us, guides us, and sanctifies us through the Word of God. Let us embrace what God has given us.

Prayer: Father of all love and truth and grace, Your Word is precious to us. Thank you so much for your love letter. Grant us to love You more and love your Word more. In Jesus' name, amen.

Defending God's Word

Attacks on God's Word

Watch the news lately? The Word of God is under siege. It is being surrounded and attacked on every side. But this is nothing new. Shortly after God gave His Words to Adam and Eve, the devil, that old serpent, tried to put doubt about what God said into the mind of Eve, and he succeeded! After God told Adam that he could not eat of the tree of good and evil, the devil came along and started chatting up Eve. He started out by saying, *"Did God really say...?"* Then he contradicted God when he said, *"No! You will not die."* And finally, the devil implied that God was evil by withhold the good stuff from Adam and Eve, *"In fact, God know that when you eat it your eyes will be opened and you will be like God."* (Genesis 3:1-4). And this attack on God, His goodness, and His Word continues down to this very day. It is being attacked in many ways on many fronts.

Is science really science?

Scientists have been attacking the Bible ever since they decided to agree that only the natural universe exists; and they think they can figure it out without God. Science by definition today discounts the spiritual aspect of life, even when they observe it. Of course, not all scientists follow the nature-only theory of the universe. There are hundreds of scientists who disagree with this theory, Christians and otherwise.

This materialistic view of science is just the opposite of the beginning of scientific study where the leading scientists were Christians and were trying to discover all that God had done. Now, according to this relatively new definition of science, if it is not according to known natural laws, they disavow it, not realizing that the natural laws we have discovered were designed and, since designed, there is in fact a Designer who doesn't exist in time, space, and matter, i.e., God. In other words, they reject the Creator and claim the creation for themselves. Their presuppositions reject God before any study begins. This is nothing more than intellectual sleight of hand.

Personal Feelings and God

Another attack on God and His Word is the use of personal feelings. Every generation has its own attacks. These days in America, transgenderism and homosexuality are big issues today with the Biden administration pushing these agendas. All this is based on personal feelings, not moral truth. One can have feelings for someone, but that doesn't make the feeling right or truthful. In Romans chapter one, God shows that people who desire aberrant variations of the man-woman relationship norm became this way because they rejected God and His way. So, God gives them up to these things. In other words, He let them do their own thing, full of sin and outright rebellion against God's way. All societies have pushed against the Word of God and this is one of the many ways the American society pushes against God.

Gobbledygook

Another attack on God's Word is the simple fact that the natural man cannot receive or even understand the things of the Spirit. (I Corinthians 2:14). So, people think the Bible is gobbledygook. They reject it out of hand since they believe it doesn't pertain to life. They are under the impression that the Bible is an ancient book of fables and stories and is useless for today's life.

And still another attack again God's Word are the God haters. These are the people who hate God, usually from some life trauma, and when He is brought up in conversation, the person lashes out against any idea of a good God. They deep down believe there is a God, but they hate Him. They hate God because they have swallowed the devil's bait that God isn't good. Often, it's because of a tragedy in one's life that he blames God for.

There may be more attacks, but this should suffice us to realize that we need to be able to defend the Word of God. By defending the Word of God, I mean we need to be able to articulate why we believe what we believe. The Bible says we *"must contend for the faith."* (Jude 3) and *"but honor the Messiah as Lord in your hearts. Always be ready to give a defense to anyone who asks you for a reason for the hope that is in you."* (I Peter 3:15) The Spirit of God will show the truth of what we say.

All Christians Can and Should Defend the Faith

The Word of God was written by the Holy Spirit He used men to write it down. (Luke 1:70; Act 1:16; 2 Timothy 3:16; 2 Peter 1:21) .He didn't have to. There are an infinite number of ways He could have given us His word. He chose to use godly men. And now He has chosen to use godly men and women to defend His Word. He chose you and me.

As royalty and priests of the Most High God (I Peter 2:9). we are meant to proclaim the praise of Him who called us *"out of darkness into His glorious light."* This means we are to bear witness to the truth of God and His Word. In fact, the word 'apologetics' comes from the Greek word for giving a logical defense of what we believe and why we believe.

We are to bear witness to all of God's Word, not just the nice parts, but the warnings and judgements as well. Jesus came into the world to save sinners. (Luke 1:77; 19:10). He gave counsel to the whole Word of God. His first public words as recorded in Matthew 4:17 *"Repent for the kingdom of Heaven of at hand."* And Mark records Jesus as saying, *"The time is fulfilled, and the kingdom of God is at hand. Repent, and believe the good news."* Jesus didn't put band aids on cancer patients. He wanted to heal souls, not just make them feel good.

Jesus was humble, full of compassion and mercy to all those who were seeking God. But to those who were defending their turf, protecting their selfish sins, He used words of judgement hoping that they would see their sins as terrible affronts to a holy God and repent. He loved them enough to die for them and knew that they needed to hear about their sins. Jude says, *"Have mercy on those who doubt; save others by snatching them from the fire; have mercy on others but with fear, hating even the garment defiled by the flesh."* (verses 22-23).

Compassion and Truth Go Hand in Hand

We are to follow in Jesus' steps. He was led by the Spirit and had compassion and mercy for all, yet He treated each one differently. He treated each one according to their needs. I personally have asked probably hundreds of Christians how they got saved. I have never had a person say the same thing as another person. Me included! When we tell people about the Kingdom of God, we must meet them where they are. We must be led by the Spirit of God and not by our external judgements.

We are God's spokespeople on earth. We are to proclaim God's Word in its entirety. Jesus did that. He was God's spokesman on Earth. And they killed Him. Now, we are to proclaim the goodness, love and forgiveness of God through Christ. We are now the light of the world according to Jesus. (Matthew 5:14).

In today's world, just like the age of the early Christians, people condemn us for our beliefs. As you can tell, attacks on Christians are multiplying here in the U.S. of A. People think Christians are the problem. If only those Christians would agree that this is okay or that is okay, the world would be better! An example of this was on the news today. The mayor of Seattle, WA blamed the Christians who were legally holding a rally and were assaulted by the LGBT community! This LBGT assault was illegal, but the mayor blamed the Christians! Sounds like, "throw them to the tigers" to me.

When we share the truth, many of these folks who attack Christians will get saved! Paul said in I Corinthians 6:9-11, *"Don't you know that the unrighteous will not inherit God's kingdom? Do not be deceived: No sexually immoral people, idolaters, adulterers, or anyone practicing homosexuality, no thieves, greedy people, drunkards, verbally abusive people, swindlers will inherit God's kingdom. And SOME OF YOU USED TO BE LIKE THIS. But you were washed, you were sanctified, you were justified in the name of the Lord Jesus Christ and by the Spirit of our God."* Praise God, there is hope!

But many others will reject what you say and hate you and hurt you. Jesus said, *"Blessed are those who are persecuted for righteousness' sake, for theirs are the kingdom of heaven. Blessed are you when they revile and persecute you and say all kinds of evil against you falsely for My sake. Rejoice and be exceedingly glad, for great is your reward in heaven, for so they persecuted the prophets who were before you*." Matthew 5:10-12).

So, defending the Word of God, which is the truth of the universe, is not for chickens, it is for warriors of the cross. Jesus told us to take up our cross and follow Him. We are not called to be weak-willed namby-pambies. We are called to hold forth the word of life and to shine as lights in this world of darkness. (Philippians 2:15-16).

Justin Martyr, who got saved while walking the beach when an old man approached him and they discussed philosophy, the Bible and life, wrote a defense of the faith to the Roman emperor Antoninus. Justin was the first noted Christian apologist. Justin was beheaded for his faith; hence Justin got the word, martyr, added to his name – Justin Martyr.

Defending the Truth

How do we defend the Word of God? The first way to defend the truth is by holy living. We should never forget that a key ingredient in defending the truth is a holy and good life. For if we don't live a holy and good life, why would people ask us about the hope we have? And when we are asked about that peculiar hope, we have to be able to give a coherent answer.

We can do deep studies in apologetics, research all the areas of philosophy, archaeology, bibliology, geology, etc. which, thank God, many capable Christian scientists do! Youtube and other outlets are full of Christians successfully defending the faith.

We should educate ourselves as well. But most important is that we should know the Bible intimately. We need to meditate on the Words of God. We need a clear, spiritual understanding of God and His ways. Then we, too, can come to the defense of the Word of God. We must remember that when we are defending God's Word, we are helping the world understand that God is good and salvation is offered freely.

It is not enough to say, "God said it; I believe it." The reason people use this expression is that most of us don't really know what God says, and we use this type of sentence as a catch phrase to deflect all arguments, sincere or otherwise. This is unacceptable. I Peter 3:15 says, *"But honor the Messiah as Lord in your hearts. Always be ready to give a defense to anyone who asks you for a reason for the hope that is within you."*

We must be ready to give a sound reason our beliefs. Our beliefs about God, Jesus, the Bible and the world around us. For example, Psalm 19 gives an excellent explanation why people should believe there is a God and His character is good. Regarding science, Isaiah 40:22 and Job 36:7 show the earth as round and suspended in the sky. These were written thousands of years before science was developed enough to find evidence for that.

Another example is Matthew Maury, the founder of modern oceanography who discovered currents in the ocean and vastly reduced ship travel times. His scientific research to find currents in the ocean was based, he told his family, on Psalm 8:8 *"The fowl of the air, and the fish of the sea, and whatsoever passeth through the paths of the seas."* (KJV). He sought out those 'paths of the seas' and found them!

There are many more examples of evidence for God and the veracity of His Word. But the biggest evidence for God is what He did for you! Be ready to share your testimony and tell people what Jesus did for you.

And stand up for the truth of God's Word. Sin is sin. True, homosexuality is a choice, but it also is a sin. Gossip is sin, so are promiscuity and drunkenness and pride and idolatry. Be firm just as Jesus was firm when He told those Sadducees that there was an afterlife and judgement was real. (They really didn't like Him for that!) Or when He told the Pharisees (those self-righteous church goers). that God desired mercy and not sacrifice. If fact He ticked them off so much with the truth that they conspired to kill Him.

Many folks don't want to offend people so instead they offend God. Let's not be like that.

One of the many results of defending the truth in our culture is rejoicing in pain and suffering. The apostle Paul had much to rejoiced about, so many thousands coming to a new life in Christ and living with peace and joy and righteousness. But he also suffered greatly; stoning, beatings, conspiracies against his life and finally jail and death.

In Luke 12:4-5 Jesus said, *"And I say to you, My friends, don't fear those who kill the body, and after that can do nothing more. But I will show you the One to fear; Fear Him who has the authority to throw people into hell after death. Yes, I say to you, this is the One to fear."* So, let us not worry about placating the feelings of those who like to live in sin. Let us hold forth the truths of God in a clear and loving way.

The Cost of Defending God's Word

We may be called upon to sacrifice all: *"Then Jesus said to His disciples, 'If anyone wants to come with Me, he must deny himself, take up his cross, and follow Me. For whoever wants to save his life will lose it, but whoever loses his life because of Me will find it. What will it benefit a man if he gains the whole world yet loses his life?'"* The early church defended

God's Word by not sacrificing to Caesar and not calling him lord. They died, terrible deaths. Through the centuries thousands upon thousands of died defending the truth as it is in Jesus. Christians are being put to death this very day simply because they are Christians.

We may or may not sacrifice to this degree, but we will sacrifice.

We should also remember that when we speak against the cultural lies and present the truth that we are ambassadors for God and we are simply giving the world His message. Jesus also said in Luke 10:16, *"Whoever listens to you listens to Me. Whoever rejects you rejects Me. And whoever rejects Me rejects the One who sent Me."*

You, Christian, are of royal blood; you are a royal priesthood. You are light for the world; you are an ambassador for Christ Himself. You are called to hold forth the Word of Life. If you care about God and care about people, you will fulfill your duty and defend God's Word.

Prayer: Father God, help us to always show Your goodness and the truth of Your Word to those lost souls who need it. To the glory of Jesus, we pray. Amen.

Sharing God's Word

You are a Priest.

Most people seem to think that sharing God's Word is up to the pastor on Sunday morning. He gets in the pulpit and delivers a message based on some Scripture. However, the Apostle Peter said in I Peter 2:9, *"But you are a chosen race, a royal priesthood, a holy nation, a people for His possession, so that you may proclaim the praises of the One who called you out of darkness into His marvelous light."* Peter was talking to every believer. According to God, we all are priests.

What does a priest do? He ministers to those around him by telling them about God's Way and by praying to God for them. That's what Moses' brother, Aaron, did. That's what the Levites did as well. Are we doing that? Are we proclaiming His promises, His praises? Are we praying for those around us?

We proclaim things all the time. Did you ever find a restaurant that was excellent? More than likely, you went back and told your friends all about it; how good the food tasted, how beautiful the inside looked, how nice and professional the staff were. And it was easy to tell people! You brought it up in conversations without hesitation as you told them what you saw, how you felt, and so on. At least, that's what I do. Isn't it ironic that most Christians, 61% according to Lifeway Research, did not share the gospel in the last six months. That's 180 days that they were around people who needed the Savior and did not tell even one of them. How many of the remaining 39% share the gospel more than once every six months is another question.

It is ironic that we can get excited about the restaurant we went to, but for some reason, we have trouble sharing the Bread of Life.

I don't think this is what our Lord intended. We are supposed to make the most of every opportunity as the Apostles tell us. *"Therefore, as we have opportunity, we must work for the good of all, especially for those who belong to the household of faith."* (Galatians 6:10). *"Act wisely toward outsiders, making the most of the time. Your speech should always be gracious, seasoned with salt, so that you may know how you should answer each person."* (Colossians 4:5-6). *"but honor the Messiah as Lord in your hearts. Always be ready to give a defense to anyone who asks you for a reason for the hope that is in you."* (I Peter 3:15). And finally, *"Have mercy on those who doubt; save others by snatching them from the fire; have mercy on others but with fear, hating even the garment defiled by the flesh."* (Jude 22,23).

Be the Good Samaritan

God's Word was given not just for us, not just for our benefit, but for the world. The Lord told us to love our neighbor as we love ourselves (Matthew 22:39). That means we are to care for our neighbors physically and spiritually. Sharing God's Word brings light and life to our neighbors. This is part of our priestly duties.

And when we share God's Word, we are to share God's Word rightly, with the right attitude in the right way. The right attitude means that we must love the person we are sharing with.

If we don't have love when we share the Word of God, we are like a noisy mosquito, just buzzing around annoying people. Also, it is the Word of God we are sharing, not just our own ideas. The Word of God is the Sword of the Spirit. It cuts to the heart. We are, in a sense, performing surgery on our neighbor to bless and heal those who need healing and to encourage those who need encouragement.

So, we should try to use the Word of God with precision. A surgeon doesn't cut open the chest to perform knee surgery. (Well, not the good ones at least!). He diagnoses the conditions and does what he thinks is best to fix it. That's how we should share God's Word.

In order to do this, we must know the Word enough so that the Holy Spirit can guide us to the right passage, to apply the right healing salve to bring healing to your neighbor and those around us. The Holy Spirit uses our minds and if the Word of God isn't stored in the mind, there is nothing for the Holy Spirit to access. We should learn and meditate on the Word of God.

Let us rely on the Great Physician to help those in need. Are they saved? Do they need encouragement? Do they need warning? Do they need comfort? These are some of the things we need to be on the lookout for as we serve the people Christ died for. And always ask for the Spirit's guidance. He knows their hearts, their hurts, their sufferings, their needs. Let Him guide you.

We must be aware of the Holy Spirit's unction. Sometimes we are led to speak with a person and sometimes to give a word of knowledge. At times, God will put that gentle urge in us to talk to the person at the other table in a restaurant, etc. And sometimes He gives us a word of knowledge on what to tell another soul. The leading of the Holy Spirit is always gentle, never oppressive. That's how we can know that it is the Holy Spirit leading us and not just some false spirit or feeling.

The sharing of the Word of God must be accompanied by the good deeds that gives the evidence that we are priests of God. James says, *"What good is it, my brothers, if someone says he has faith but does not works? Can that faith save him?"* And a little later he says, *"I will show you faith from my works".* (James 2:14,18b). So, when we share the Word of God, we must be able to back up what the Bible says by helping our neighbor whenever we can.

The sharing of God's Word, which brings life, must be shared with grace. Jesus came to us full of "*grace and truth".* (John 1:17). And Colossians 4:6 says, *"Your speech should always be gracious, seasoned with salt, so that you may know how you should answer each person."* We need to be pleasant to talk to, not like some who shout the Word of God as if they were throwing stones instead of offering the Bread of Life. As much as in us is, we must be gracious. After all, how does Jesus talk to us? Jesus is a straight shooter; He tells it like it is, but He does it with grace, lots and lots of grace. James 3:18 says, *"And the fruit of righteousness is sown in peace by those to cultivate peace."*

Psalm 45 makes this point very clear. Verses three through six, *"Gird your sword upon your side, O mighty one; clothe yourself with splendor and majesty. In your majesty, ride forth victoriously on behalf of truth, humility and righteousness; let your right hand display awesome deeds. Let your sharp arrows pierce the hearts of the king's enemies; let the nations fall beneath your feet. Your throne, O God, will last for ever and ever; a scepter of justice will be the scepter of your kingdom"* (NIV). In the midst of this great and wonderful saying which expresses the awesome power of God's man on earth, the word humility at first doesn't seem to fit. This all-powerful man, who subdues kingdoms and nations, who has his sword at his side, who works for truth and righteousness, also works for humility. God is humble.

Isn't that strange; the most powerful man is the most humble as well. He has right and justice on his side and he knows the exact ways of right and justice, but he doesn't lord it over us, though he has that authority. He is humble.

I need to remember that though I know the truth and right and wrong, and though I know the way of righteousness, I must be humble and not use that knowledge to harm but to help.

Sharing the Word of God gives light for living. Jesus said we are the light of the world. (Matthew 5:14). The rest of the world lives out their lives in darkness, being deceived, looking for fulfillment, looking for purpose in life, and finding emptiness.

We have the Way; we have the light! We can show people how to know God and find purpose! Also, we have the bread of life, we have eternal nourishment for everyone! And the world is starving because there is a famine in the land. There is a famine of the Word of God. As one preacher put it, sharing God's Word is like one beggar telling another beggar where to find food. We have eternal food.

We must share with those around us who are groping in the darkness and hungry for life. The signs of this darkness and famine are clearly evident around us every day. People are trying to find fulfillment. A few of the ways they try are materialism, selfishness, religion, activities and many other ways. Many have given up and just want to party to hide their despair. Romans chapters one, two and three cover this very well. All of these are either looking for life or giving up on life. We have Life. We have Light, We have the true Bread from Heaven. Let's share.

As it says in Colossians, we should always be ready to share the Good News. (Colossians 4:6). Sometimes when we least expect it, God uses us to minister to others. For example, many times I have said something that sparked a reaction of inquiry. I didn't feel led to say it, I had no prompting to say it. It was me being me and God using me to reach someone. Once at the local Dollar Tree, the checkout lady asked me how I was. I responded with the word "Happy!" She asked me why.

Right then I had the thought, "Should I say because it is a good day or should I say because Jesus died for my sins and forgave me and that's why I happy." I chose the latter. The gentleman standing behind me said He wanted that. So, after he made his purchase, we moved aside and he told me his story that he had made a confession of Christ in prison, but that he wasn't really sincere. Now he wanted the Savior for real this time. So, we prayed and he got saved! This, of course, was totally unexpected for me. I certainly didn't plan on leading someone to the Lord by responding with 'happy'. But that is what happened.

Another time when I was working second shift at this factory, a fellow worker who was younger, bold, and had made a mess of his life so far, asked me why God used Mary to have Jesus. (He thought that was odd and not the best way.). Well, we had been working overtime for many days and I was tired, so I responded, "What's it to you how God used that method to bring Jesus into the world?" I didn't really say it in a kind and tender manner and I thought I blew my witness with him. But a few days later, he mentioned to me that that was the best answer He ever heard about that! Those are wonderful events when God uses us without our knowing. But more often God uses us when we do know and are actively seeking to share Him through His Word.

As priests, it is our duty to share God's Word, as a brother or sister to Christ, it is our privilege to share God's Word, and as saved sinners, it is our joy to share God's Word. Remember Romans 10:17, *"So faith comes from hearing, and hearing by the Word of Christ."* And let's remember the verse before this one, *"How beautiful are the feet of those who bring good news of good things!"* (Romans 10:9). I always remember Rick Frey and Mike Cooper who took the time to stop by my place and got me to go to church. I got saved that day and whenever I see Rick, I remind him of the good work he did. Once he told me that I always bring that up. I answered that, of course, I do!

When we share God's Word, we should keep in mind that we are sharing The Word, that is God in the flesh, Jesus Himself. If we just share theological points or nice illustrations about being nice, are we really sharing God's Word? Unfortunately, most churches never share the Good News and how to be saved in their services. Jesus Himself said, *"You examine the Scriptures because you think that in them you have eternal life; and it is those very Scriptures that testify about Me;"* (John 5:39). So, when we share the Word of God as good stewards, we must share Christ. Otherwise, it would be like talking about apple pie but never mentioning apples! Just doesn't work.

So, dear reader, be ready to give an answer. Do the best you can and let the Spirit of Jesus do the rest. And just think how much more God can use you when you have the Word of God firmly established in your heart.

Do you remember how you got saved? How you found out about God's Way? How happy you were? Let's pass that on. Let's share the Message of the Messiah.

Prayer: Father of light, forgive us for not sharing your Word as Your Son told us to. Please put into our hearts so much love for You and our neighbors that we share Your Good News of redemption in Jesus, Your Way to eternal life. Amen.

Made in the USA
Middletown, DE
19 July 2025